MW01503022

HIS BROTHER'S KEEPER

50 Years
of the American Jewish Society for Service

HIS BROTHER'S KEEPER

50 YEARS

OF THE AMERICAN JEWISH SOCIETY FOR SERVICE

Paul Milkman

With a Foreword by
Jacob Neusner

Academic Studies in the History of Judaism
Global Publications, Binghamton University
2001

Copyright © 2001 by Paul Milkman

Publication Data:

Author: Paul Milkman
Title: His Brother's Keeper: 50 Years of the American Jewish Society for Service
ISBN: 1-58684-105-X

Published and Distributed by:
Academic Studies in the History of Judaism
Global Publications, Binghamton University
State University of New York at Binghamton
LNG 99, Binghamton University
Binghamton, New York, USA 13902-6000
Phone: (607) 777-4495 or 777-6104; Fax: (607) 777-6132
Email: pmorewed@binghamton.edu
http://ssips.binghamton.edu

ACADEMIC STUDIES
IN THE HISTORY OF JUDAISM

Publisher: Global Publications, State University of New York at Binghamton
Address: LNG 99, SUNY-Binghamton, Binghamton, New York 13902-6000

This book is dedicated to Henry Kohn,
who has broadened the horizons of two thousand young people,
And to Catherine and Caitlyn, who share AJSS adventures with me

TABLE OF CONTENTS

ABOUT THE AUTHOR

Paul Milkman is the author of *PM: A New Deal in Journalism, 1940-1948* (Rutgers University Press, 1997). He was educated in the New York City public schools, the City College of New York, Hunter College and Rutgers University, where he received his PhD in History in 1994. A teacher since 1972, he has taught history at Rutgers, John Jay College of Criminal Justice, and Long Island University. He has been a teacher of English at Midwood High School in Brooklyn since 1987. Director of Camp Thoreau from 1979-1989, he is now a Project Director for the American Jewish Society for Service, which brings teenagers to work as volunteers in building or improving low income housing in cooperation with non-profit organizations throughout the United States.

Foreword

The American Jewish Society for Service celebrates its fiftieth year, an event in the history of Judaism. For half a century the Society has realized in concrete deeds the prophetic vision for the social order, a vision of service to the needy, of *tzedakah*, the Hebrew word for righteousness and also for charity. But that service takes the form not of donating funds, an impersonal, generic action, but of donating one's own strength and energy, personally and particularly. Giving a month and a half or more for five eight-hour days a week to build, paint, renovate, clean up, the young people gathered in the Society's projects have gotten as much as they have given. The experience of hard work for others carries with it lessons learned for a lifetime.

Paul Milkman tells that story in the pleasing manner of a professional writer, but with the rigorous attention to fact and detail of a scholar. The book graces this series under my editorship, in an academic press's imprint, for three reasons.

First and most important, here is a reliable record of an exemplary activity motivated by Judaism and representative of a broadly-held Judaic ideal. Just as the academic study of Judaism finds its data in the prayers that people offer or the holy days they celebrate and holy deeds they carry out, so that study values the story of how the religious teachings shape concrete actions in the workaday world. If people want to know, what is it that Jews do by reason of their faith, and how do their deeds realize that faith, here is an account that answers that fundamental question.

Second, Dr. Milkman himself places his narrative into the very center of the Judaic religious situation. The way in which he accounts for the organization and its activity leaves no doubt that Judaism, in a particular formulation, animates the program. The way in which he describes, analyzes, and interprets the half-century of service establishes the context, religious aspiration, not merely social service. The opening chapter provides a thumbnail sketch of the Judaic, not merely the ethnic-Jewish, situation in mid-century America. His is a sociology of religion, not solely of the Jews as an ethnic group.

Third, Dr. Milkman spells out the specific religious aspiration and theological motivation that yielded the founding of the Society and guided its program: Reform Judaism fully realized in action. Rabbi Ferdinand Isserman had the imagination to translate prophetic idealism into social activism:

> "Slums, poverty, war, unemployment inflict pain. Such pain
> is not cosmic. It is imposed by man, man-made. It can be avoided. It is

> an evidence of social injustice, or lack of spiritual sensitiveness and moral will on the part of people . . . The emphasis of success for self, if need be, at the expense of the community, the *laissez-faire* policy of extreme individualism, has brought our nation to the brink of the abyss.

Then there was Rabbi Arthur Lelyveld, pioneer in the struggle against racism as a project in the service of God, the perfection of creation as God's partner:

> To 'perfect the world,'[is] to struggle for the elimination of selfishness, greed, lack of concern for others, corruption, violence and war. It is, in other words, the leap from individual priority into a worldview that holds the vision of a redeemed society and commits us to enlist in the cause of bringing that society about.

Active in the Jewish peace movement and in Jewish youth work, ultimtely as national director of the Hillel Foundations in the service of Jewish university students, Lelyveld possessed a clear vision of what the active participant in the social order had to do. He was one of the those who put his life on the line in the civil rights revolution of the 1960s. The third in the trilogy of Jewish figures Milkman introduces in his account of the opening of the Society for Service, is Isidor Hoffman, Jewish chaplain at Columbia University and founder of the Jewish Peace Fellowship. These three recognized as their model the American Friends Service Committee, a sectarian Quaker group, and, as proud and self-respecting Jews and practitioners of Judaism, they aspired to a Judaic counterpart. That was a natural initiative, considering that half of the AFSC volunteers were Jewish to begin with.

The catalyst for action was a disciple of Rabbi Isserman, Henry Kohn, a lawyer by profession, a Jew by vocation. He took the vision of the prophets as mediated by the rabbis and turned it into an effective institution, an organization with a program and a budget to realize that program. His was the kind of leadership that insisted on engagement with the substance of matters, not the kind that raises the funds and hires "professionals."

That is what makes the story of the Society for Service compelling: how people made of theology a practical program, and one that aimed at changing the world. The account of how Henry Kohn translated the ideals of Reform Judaism into a working organization with an effective program fills the pages of this book, which I am proud to include in an academic series devoted to the history of Judaism. That history, it is clear in Dr. Milkman's narrative, records success in realizing precisely the goals that animated the initiative to begin with. And that is a story that cannot be told too many times.

Jacob Neusner

Research Professor of Religion and Theology
Senior Fellow of the Institute of Advanced Theology
Bard College

Preface

The vast horizon of the Wyoming sky barely hinted at evening as 16 Jewish teenagers, their counselors, and project directors departed from Riverton's modern St. John's Lutheran Church at 6:00 PM in late July 1998. For four weeks, the young people had slept on sleeping bags in carpeted rooms normally operated during the school year as classrooms. They had used the modern kitchen and dining room of the church for breakfast and dinner and also prepared the next day's bag lunches there. To bathe after days of heavy, sweaty labor, they had showered at the large, perfectly appointed high school swimming pool a mile away. Now they had driven back to the church only to change into the cleanest and dressiest clothes they had brought with them: button down plaid shirts instead of tees, clean jeans replacing those caked with sweat and mud, sneakers instead of work boots.

The church faced an open field that gave perfect views for western panoramas, but by now these urban and suburban youngsters, mostly from the northeast (though California, Florida, and Missouri were represented in the group), no longer stopped to admire the scenery. Instead they piled into three minivans - two brand new rented vehicles and "Libby," an ancient Toyota minivan with nearly 300,000 miles registered on the odometer, donated for the summer by a perfect stranger from the Casper, Wyoming Jewish congregation and named by the teenagers after the fictional terrorists who threaten Doc Brown in *Back to the Future*. Though the new vans were air conditioned and still boasted excellent suspension, the young people preferred the open windows and bumpy ride of the older vehicle.

In two or three short blocks, the three cars reached Main Street and turned towards downtown, passing the ubiquitous fast food establishments and the two single screen movie theatres, each over 50 years old. This Main Street did have its unique features: several stores selling handicrafts made by the local Arapaho and Shoshone tribes who share the Wind River Indian Reservation. Turning right twice, the vehicles entered "Indian territory." Now the horizon was vaster still, for it was encumbered only by a few scattered buildings. Most of the land under the great sky is untamed grass; much of it is dotted in summer by green fuzz on otherwise bare brown earth. At random intervals groups of old and beaten cars surround homes, many of them worn and dilapidated trailers.

Two or three more turns placed the cars on dusty unpaved road; in less than a mile the vehicles parked at their destination. The contingent walked into an unusual establishment: a half-completed straw bale house. For four weeks the young people had worked from 8AM to 4 PM on, in and around stacked barley straw bales, turning what had once been considered agricultural waste into a three bedroom home. They had placed and secured windows and doors, built wooden soffets, fully drywalled and "mudded" the ceiling and interior walls of rooms, removed nails from wood for reuse and toted stones to prepare for landscaping. While most home construction requires similar effort, the teenagers had also engaged in a unique activity. The bales, the basis for the exterior walls of the entire house, had to be shaved for evenness and encased in chicken wire, which would eventually hold in place the clay-like material to create an adobe home. The chicken wire itself needed to tightly encase the bales; to accomplish this, groups of two had exchanged a three foot iron "needle" threaded with wire, which was knotted and passed through two feet of straw from exterior to interior of the house and back outside again.

After four weeks of their labor, the house had taken shape. It was no longer the odd group of straw bales which looked like a giant's Lego set; instead it was a few steps away from being a finished building. Unfortunately, the group would not be around to see the building completed; scheduling difficulties made it uncertain when the adobe would be applied, and the following day the contingent would be moving to Casper where they would spread two weeks of effort at a half-dozen sites.

These young people were at work in the 48th summer of the American Jewish Society for Service. Thousands of teenagers have worked since 1951 in seven and six week programs, building, renovating and painting housing, playgrounds, community centers, and parks. They have hooked up with a variety of community, government and church organizations, donating unpaid labor to provide economically disadvantaged Americans with vital resources. In self-created Friday evening services they have understood this activity as a way of defining themselves as Americans and as Jews, believing that service for others is a mandatory component of a meaningful life. They have worked in 45 of the continental United States in over 120 projects.

The volunteers have paid tuition to fund their supervision, their food, and their travel. While working full five-day weeks, they have explored their local communities during the evenings and traveled several hundred mile distances on the weekends to immerse themselves in whatever portion of the nation they have journeyed to. The Wyoming group had already spent one weekend in Yellowstone and another at Grand Teton National Park; during their Casper stay, they would gaze at Mount Rushmore while camping out in Custer State Park in the South Dakota Black Hills.

To understand their environment, they had listened to the executive director of Wind River Habitat for Humanity, the summer project host, speak of her organization's mission and been taught Arapaho songs, games and drum dances. They had volunteered for an evening of card games and talk at the reservation nursing home. They toured the only completed straw bale house in Riverton, a model for their present work, and visited a farmer whose barley crop, harvested by the beer companies, could make straw available for home construction. There, they listened to a discussion of water shortages and practiced irrigating fields. In both Riverton and Casper they attended semi-professional theater in local college auditoriums.

But the evening ahead was perhaps the most meaningful of all. Through all of the labor at the straw bale house, the work supervisor had been none other than the homeowner, 28 year old Mike Monroe. A roving fire fighter, who normally travels to the worst hot spots in the country during the summer, Monroe had devoted himself to creating his own home, far exceeding the normal sweat equity requirement imposed by Habitat. His calm patience had guided the unskilled workers. During lunch breaks, Monroe and his brother had taught Arapaho games and dances. His wife Laura, who defied cerebral palsy to pursue her Masters degree in social work and returned to the reservation to open a center to treat children of domestic abuse, spent an evening describing her work and had arranged for the group to visit the Catholic center on the reservation. The Monroe's two young boys and their dauschund, Hobo, had been frequent visitors to the worksite.

The first supper ever served in the new Monroe home was shared with the AJSS group. The food was prepared by Catherine Kaczmarek Milkman, project director. Habitat director Cathy Yoccheim distributed Habitat hats to everyone in attendance. Paul and Catherine Milkman brought the traditional bread, wine, and salt to symbolize the nurturance of home, and the group presented the Monroes with a welcome mat for the new front door. Mike and Laura reciprocated. Each girl camper received a pair of beaded earrings, an example of Arapaho handicrafts, while the boys were given beaded key chains. The Monroes presented Catherine and me with a hand-sewn quilt embroidered with a traditional Arapaho design.

We would see the Monroes again when they journeyed to Casper to take part in our final banquet before the group departed from Wyoming. But that night, as the group left the straw bale house, the lights in the campers' eyes were reflected by the brilliant stars illuminating the broad sky. The meaning of that evening is at the core of 50 years of activity.

Few organizations enable young people to give of themselves as fully as does the American Jewish Society for Service. Six solid weeks of meaningful labor in eight hour days for five days a week is the normal workload. Campers are also given a crash course about the locality in which they work and the beauty of the country that surrounds them. Additionally, they are encouraged to view their labor as helping to define their outlook in the world: This is what it means to be Jewish; this is what it means to be a responsible adult.

The history of the organization that follows is inevitably also a history of contemporary American Judaism and of domestic change in the United States during the second half of the twentieth century. It cannot be comprehensive about these larger issues, but neither can it ignore them, as they provide the context for the organization's genesis, growth, and operation. The judgments made about these social issues are entirely my own. My role as a project director also means I am not a neutral observer. In many ways, what follows is a personal story.

As the reader will discover, this book is also about the vision of three rabbis, now deceased, and the vision and persistent dedication of principal founder Henry Kohn. His unflagging leadership has continually nurtured AJSS from its founding to today. He might well disagree with some of the political conclusions here. What we share is respect for the organization he has devoted much of his life to nurturing.

1

Defining Jewish Identity in Modern America

American Jewry stood nervously in unfamiliar territory at mid-century. As a result of horrific, almost unimaginable slaughter, the United States was suddenly the population center for Judaism worldwide. Where Warsaw and Berlin had once been the home of influential Jewish cultural, political, and religious institutions, New York was now the established capital of American and international Judaism.

American Jews, however, could not exactly crow about their sudden emergence. The details of the Nazi carnage only became known at the close of the Second World War, and the Nuremberg trials of war criminals kept details publicly traumatic through 1948. While the tribunals were finishing their deliberations, the struggle to establish Israel became a new focus of public concern. The birth of that nation, surely an event the majority of American Jews celebrated, was nonetheless cause for considerable worry. As the country declared its independence, it was attacked by its neighbors. The worldwide sympathy gained from international condemnation of German atrocities did not guarantee Israel safe passage to statehood. Jews continued to feel that they must remain at attention.

Of course, one need not focus on the immediate issues of the preceding decade to remain wary. More than a millenium of anti-Semitic activity had permanently etched defensiveness, wariness, or at least caution into most Jewish brows. Here in "the golden land," indeed in "the promised city," Jews had felt the sting of intolerance. Even after war had been declared in Europe, a series of violent attacks by Christian Front hoodlums on Jewish youngsters in the Bronx, Brooklyn and Manhattan made newspaper headlines.[1]

Newspaper exposure was necessary after the victory over fascism to eliminate the scandal of quotas aimed at reducing Jewish enrollment at prestigious university undergraduate and professional schools and to force the establishment of the state university system in New York which would be publicly committed to non-sectarian admission and hiring practices.[2]

Understandable, then, was the Jewish preoccupation with matters of self-defense and survival. A host of Jewish organizations aimed at preventing anti-Semitism in the United States and lending support to tiny, embattled Israel appeared on the scene. Many of these organizations were new; other older ones were energized with new members and increased financial support.

Nonetheless, there was an unknown irony in the public awareness and battle against anti-Semitism and for survival. Not since the Babylonian destruction of the temple in ancient Jerusalem had Jews enjoyed as much success in assimilating into a relatively accepting society. Never before were so many descendants of Jacob's family as financially secure in a nation that increasingly condemned anti-Semitism and regarded its existence as a poisonous emblem of a hated and defeated enemy.

By 1950 roads to success were being constructed that the next decades would cement into place. After the great immigration wave of 1880-1920, most American Jews had been poor, proletarian urbanites; more than half lived in the five boroughs of the City of New York. The anti-Semitic hatred of "Jew York" seemed based on reality. The nation's garment industry, with manufacturing centers in New York and Chicago, were dominated by thousands of Jewish workers, who were also well represented in hundreds of New York manufacturing and transportation trades.[3]

"But Jake," asks Gitl in the film *Hester Street*[4] (from Abraham Cahan's 1896 short story *Yekl*[5]), "Where do the gentiles live in America?... Everywhere I look is Jews." Neighborhoods like Williamsburg and Brownsville gave Brooklyn a Jewish population of more than 850,000 before the Second World War; the Bronx had more than half a million Jews at the same time.[5] Jews had moved into new neighborhoods en masse, following Jewish contractors out of the Lower East Side into "outlying neighborhoods" like Brownsville.[7]

Now a new trend was beginning. Once the quota system was exposed, embarrassed bastions of WASP culture were flooded by ambitious Jewish intellectuals, applying the ancient traditions of Talmudic study to secular, worldly uses. The great symbol of American academic excellence is Harvard; by 1952 25% of its student body was Jewish. Even the old WASP enclave, Princeton, saw its barriers breached. Where only 1% of its student body had been Jewish in 1935, by the 1990s, 20% of its enrollment was Jewish. Yale had a greater percentage of Jewish students a decade earlier. Indeed, by the mid-1970s, Jews averaged 14 years of education, "a half-year more than Episcopalians, the next highest percentage." Fewer than half of Americans went to college; 80% of Jews did. By 1971, Jewish students made up 17% of American private university enrollment despite being less than 2% of the population. Nor was this penetration rate limited to the student body. Where only 2% of American professors were Jewish in 1940, 10% were Jewish thirty years later. In 1967 38% of the faculty at the nation's elite schools were Jews.[8]

Following the career paths made possible by their education, large numbers of Jews, now dominated by second and third generation descendants of the great immigration wave, entered the professions. Children of garment workers became teachers, doctors, lawyers, academics, electrical engineers, and business executives who adjusted to white collars and middle class life styles.

Edward Shapiro notes, "Historian Arthur Hertzberg estimated that, in the two decades between 1945 and 1965, one out of every three Jews left the big cities for the suburbs, a rate higher than that of other Americans." New Jersey suburbanization often seemed to be entirely at the impulse of New York area Jews. In 1948, 600 Jews lived in Millburn, 1600 in West Orange, and fewer than 100 in Livingston. In 1958 Millburn had 2000 Jews, West Orange 7000 and Livingston more than 2500. In the same ten-year period, Newark's Jewish population fell from 58,000 to 41,000. The trend was just beginning. In the 1970s alone, the Jewish population of New York City declined by one third to slightly over one million.[9] While some of these Jews were moving across the country, most were participating in the great expansion of New York's suburban area.

There was a curious paradox attending this suburban movement. When they lived in the city, only the Orthodox could be counted on for regular synagogue membership and attendance. And as their conservative, reform, and secular compatriots fled the inner city for the new suburban promised land, large numbers of newly arrived Orthodox Jews, including a massive influx of Hassidim, altered the appearance of many Jewish communities in New York. Williamsburg, Crown Heights, and Borough Park were populated by the remnants of European Jewry, holding on to their traditions with a new found zealotry fueled by the urgent need to maintain every aspect of their beliefs and folkways that Hitler had murderously attempted to extinguish.[10]

Their less religious colleagues had found synagogue membership and attendance often peripheral to their identity as Jews when they lived in urban Jewish communities surrounded by secular institutions that reified their ethnic identities. Now, their movement into the suburbs mandated membership in local temples. A host of contemporary developments eroded Jewish identity. The wasting away of the Yiddish language as the principal means of communication also caused the consequent disappearance of the Yiddish language press and the Yiddish theater. Kosher foods were now available in the supermarket instead of at the neighborhood butcher. More comfortable lifestyles (and the intimidation of the McCarthy era) made trade union politics irrelevant, and the Soviet Union's pariah status militated against Jewish socialism and communism. Zionism was transformed by its adoption by the American State Department from a revolutionary position to the focus of fund raising. There were far fewer worldly ways to maintain Jewish consciousness. Parents who had rarely been to synagogue now insisted that their children attend Hebrew school. Where in 1930 only 20% of Jewish families had been affiliated with a synagogue, 60% were members in 1960.[11]

The newfound attendance did not guarantee more worship. Though Shapiro notes that "Suburban Jews experienced a synagogue 'edifice complex' during the 1950s, 1960s, and 1970s" and that the buildings were newly impressive as they were "equipped with catering halls, classrooms, game rooms, and even miniature gymnasiums," he bemoans that these "shuls with pools and schools" were social centers, not places for religious study. The synagogues, which the orthodox flooded weekly to mark the Sabbath as the centerpiece of a 24 hour period to recognize the central place of their religion in their lives, were in the more affluent and assimilated reform and conservative suburban communities often nearly empty 51 weeks of the year. Weekly observance was replaced by yearly attendance. Jewish consciousness remained, but outside of fearing and protecting against renewed anti-Semitism—an increasingly remote threat—it was difficult to define positively.[12]

The danger that this ersatz Judaism posed was its own elimination, not as in Europe by a ferocious genocide, but by assimilation so total as to militate against a positively asserted Jewish identity. How could modern Judaism articulate a worldview which affirmatively demonstrated what it meant to be Jewish in contemporary America? Concerned Jewish intellectuals have actively grappled with this question since the end of the Second World War.

A prominent reform rabbi sought to provide the answer. Traveling from his home pulpit in St. Louis, Ferdinand M. Isserman spoke at a conclave in Cincinnati in March 1950 and identified

> "a hunger for a strong faith which characterizes this generation. Perhaps, living as we are in trying days, emerged as we have from a devastating war and from the harrowing experiences of a brutal persecution, filled as we are with forebodings of conflicts to come, we hunger for a faith to which we can cling and which will abide the storms and tempests of history."

He insisted the role of the rabbinate was to "define it [Judaism] so that others who desire may understand and perhaps experience it."[13]

Isserman had already spent more than two decades redefining and acting on a socially active view of his faith. Born in Antwerp, Belgium in March 1898, Isserman traveled to the United States with his parents in 1906. Ordained as a rabbi from Hebrew Union College in 1922, he was first installed at the Holy Blossom Temple in Toronto from 1925 to 1929. That year he moved to St. Louis, where he remained an increasingly influential rabbi until his death in 1972.[14]

A prolific writer, Isserman was a charismatic leader. He influenced a generation of confirmation students to embrace a Judaism of social justice. His theology, which he called prophetic Judaism, identified the biblical prophets—Nathan, Amos, Isaiah, Hosea, and Jeremiah—as transforming Judaism from one of "all religions [that] have beginnings in animism, in totemism, in child and animal sacrifice, in magic and in shamanism"[15] to a Judaism that fought nationalism and greed and demanded societal reform in behalf of the needy.

Isserman combined his reading of the prophets—who got their name from the Hebrew *nabi*, meaning to speak truth[16]—with a social activism born of the great depression and the struggle against fascism. His two principal philosophic texts, *Rebels and Saints* (1933) and *This is Judaism* (1944)[17] articulate a worldview that is religious and worldly, scholarly and compassionate, steeped in ancient tradition and immediately political.

The prophets, he wrote, were political revolutionaries. "Jeremiah denouncing the cult was a thousand times more heretical in his age than the wildest communist is in ours."[18] The earliest prophets, beginning with Nathan (in *2 Samuel*) fought against the complacency of ancient Israel, attacking those who basked in nationalism, greed and luxuriousness while indifferent to poverty around them.

> The prophets of Israel... advocated... a revolution of the spirit. They wanted men to become aware of the injustice of exploitation, of the immorality of crushing the poor, of the sinfulness of tolerating hunger amid plenty. They demanded social justice in the name of the God of justice and love. Moreover, they sought justice not only for the Hebrews, but also for the stranger and foreigner, for all men. In their eyes religion was not a mere part of life; it was all of life.[19]

If Jews were chosen people, it did not mean that they were privileged. As defined by Ezekial (*Isaiah* 42:1-7; 49:6), they were "chosen not for special material favors or gain, but rather for the voluntary assumption of a noble task."[20]

Much of Isserman's message seemed to cast the prophets as advocates for the victims of the twentieth century's Great Depression:

> Even as in Amos' generation, so too in our own, prosperity is not a sign of godliness. Like Amos, we have learned through bitter experience that a nation which violates the moral laws of the universe cannot avert the day of reckoning. Poverty and luxury cannot continue to live side by side. Palatial residences and miserable tenements cannot continue in our community. Increasing capital and decreasing consuming power are violations of moral as well as of economic laws.[21]

> "Slums, poverty, war, unemployment inflict pain. Such pain is not cosmic. It is imposed by man, man-made. It can be avoided. It is an evidence of social injustice, or lack of spiritual sensitiveness and moral will on the part of people . . . The emphasis of success for self, if need be, at the expense of the community, the *laissez-faire* policy of extreme individualism, has brought our nation to the brink of the abyss.[22]

The solution to the problems of poverty amid plenty could be found in the bible, too. Even earlier than the prophets, the Torah related how God told Moses: "When you reap the harvest of your land, you shall not reap your field to its very border, neither shall you gather the gleanings after your harvest. And you shall not strip your vineyard bare, neither shall you gather the fallen grapes of your vineyard; you shall leave them for the poor and for the sojourner."[23] For Isserman this clearly meant that a sweatshop operator "is violating the will of God."[24]

> Whoever would be righteous must shelter and protect the
> widow and orphan, the hungry and sick. The word *tsedekah* hints perhaps
> at the charity of the future—not the giving of relief which is temporary
> but the reform of our industrial and business procedures so that all the
> circumstances which create unemployment and want, which prematurely
> crush men, will be eliminated. Unemployment insurance, old age
> pensions, medical care, work for all are implied in the Jewish word for
> charity—*righteousness.*[25]

He was impatient with members of his congregation who tolerated social inequity, and he threatened their indifference, warning them that Jeremiah cast out sinners. Righteousness must be inborn and acted on; attendance at synagogue did not guarantee its presence:

> Sometimes as I look at a church, synagogue, and cathedral,
> as I behold the snobbishness that prevails in them, the class lines that
> are drawn in them, and the color line, too, as I see their leaders, lay and
> spiritual, put all stress on the business technique and organization; I am
> aghast, not at the apathy in religion, but at the masses who are still
> interested and who supinely tolerate this degeneration.[26]

Isserman insisted time and again that the demand for social justice was not to be restricted to Jews. Monotheism, the great theological discovery Jews gave to all people, created one moral path. A belief in one God—instead of each nation having a god to defend its unique interests—mandated a belief in one humanity. Furthermore, God told Moses, "When a stranger sojourns with you in your land, you shall not do him wrong. The stranger who sojourns with you shall be to you as the native among you, and you shall love him as yourself; for you were strangers in the land of Egypt."[27]

For Isserman this translated into being an early opponent not only of fascism in Europe (He traveled to Germany twice in the early 1930s and understood within a few months of Hitler's ascendance that Nazi rule meant mass annihilation for German Jews.[28]), but also of being an outspoken opponent of racial discrimination in the United States. "People of America, awake from your stupor! The Japanese, Chinese, Russians, Negroes, Mexicans are children of one father and one God has created them. You cannot remain indifferent to their welfare."[29] He warned Jews and all observant Americans, "Religion would not be true to itself if it denied the equality of the races."[30]

While the battle against fascism raged, Isserman presented religious social activism as humanity's hope. "Judaism proclaims from the housetops its hope and dream of a regenerated society, a commonwealth of man based on justice and brotherhood."[31] To proclaim that hope meant to act on it.

As the 1940s came to a close, Isserman found two prominent co-religionists seeking to motivate a new generation in the ideals of Judaism.

Arthur Lelyveld was only 36 years old in 1949, but he had been a prominent figure in the news in the post-war era. Although he had been ordained as a rabbi as late as 1939, he was nonetheless chosen to be the Executive Director of the Committee on Unity for Palestine in the Zionist Organization of America. He met with President Truman several times in 1947 and 1948 as the organizational voice of American Jews seeking to influence United States policy to recognize an independent Israel. The Committee on Unity was well named; the endless jokes about Jewish divisiveness have always been grounded in reality. The Talmudic tradition of debate has been translated to dozens of fissures in Jewish religious and secular organizations. Even support for an independent Israel was not guaranteed unanimous support among American Jews. Chaim Potok reminds us that among many orthodox Jews, especially among the Hasidim, an independent Israel before the coming of the Messiah was viewed as heretical and proponents of Zionism lambasted as traitors to the faith.[32]

Still, Lelyveld proved to be skilled at uniting diverse factions and voicing a relatively unified public view. After Israel's independence, he served as Executive Vice-President of the America-Israel Cultural Foundation, seeking to again unite diverse branches of Judaism to aid and support the new, embattled state.

He believed that to unite Jews, one must provide them with a stirring faith. "What we must seek in every branch of a uniquely pluralistic American Judaism is the production of earnest, learned, and sincerely devoted Jews, committed to the building of a more perfect world."

Like Isserman, Lelyveld believed the source of this impulse lay in religious tradition. In *The Steadfast Stream*, he wrote that to understand "the participation of Jews in movements of social betterment," one must "trace its relevance to the Jewish concern for truth and equity, integrity and peace, compassion and the goal of a just society."

> These add up to a 'value stance' that is founded in and motivated by religious conviction... I believe that normative Judaism lays particular emphasis on social righteousness as that which represents its cult and its culture, its ethic and its relationship to the Divine...
> To 'perfect the world,'[is] to struggle for the elimination of selfishness, greed, lack of concern for others, corruption, violence and war. It is, in other words, the leap from individual priority into a worldview that holds the vision of a redeemed society and commits us to enlist in the cause of bringing that society about.[33]

A more perfect world began in America. Lelyveld, like Isserman, was devoted to eliminating racism in the United States. Both men served on local boards of the NAACP – Isserman in St. Louis and Lelyveld in Cleveland – long before civil rights became a centerpiece of the mainstream liberal agenda. Like Isserman, he traced his opposition to racism to biblical sources. "I do not serve the cause of

Negro emancipation because I expect the Negro to love me in return. The command to remember the stranger and oppressed is unconditional." Perhaps he identified with pioneering against intolerance. At Columbia University as an undergraduate, he had been the first Jewish editor-in-chief of the *Spectator.*

Later, when the civil rights movement intensified, Lelyveld traveled to Mississippi. During the voter registration drive in 1964, he was attacked and beaten in Hattiesburg. He was the natural choice to deliver the eulogy for slain civil rights worker Andrew Goodman.

Lelyveld's activism was animated by his perspective on the activities of the prophets. "Amos' preaching at Beth-El put him in danger of his life. Isaiah led protest demonstrations in Jerusalem, and Jeremiah was arrested and persecuted for his public demonstrations and resistance to authority."[34]

Fifteen years before, as National Director of B'Nai B'rith Hillel, he sought an organizational alternative to channel youthful Jewish idealism.[35] His work in Hillel and in the Jewish peace movement brought him into contact with Isidor Hoffman, who spent most of his adult career as a youth counselor at Cornell and Columbia, from which he graduated in 1920. Hoffman was a reconstructionist conservative rabbi, not reform, as were Isserman and Lelyveld; but like them he held that commitment to righteousness meant helping the stranger and oppressed, and like them he saw mid-century as a turning point requiring an organizational expression for Jewish humanitarianism.[36]

Moreover, Hoffman, too, was drawn to prophetic Judaism; he had already created an organizational embodiment for his own radical political views. Hoffman read the prophet Isaiah's condemnation of inequity and war as a clarion call for pacifist politics. Indeed, he held to those views even as most Jews enthusiastically embraced violence during the Second World War. Originally the leader of a Jewish contingent within the War Resister's League, Hoffman grew increasingly disenchanted with the WRL's single-minded pursuit of draft resistance. Instead, he advocated a pacifist ideal that recommended a variety of alternate service opportunities and which struggled to alter those inequalities in international society which fostered war. In 1943, he led his disaffected faction out of the War Resisters League to create the Jewish Peace Fellowship, with which he remained active until his death in 1981. His advocacy of ending social inequity made him one of the few Jewish leaders to call for a binational – Jewish and Palestinian – state when Israel was created, and his organization has consistently advocated respect for the Palestinian population ever since. He was a steadfast opponent of the Vietnam war twenty years later. He also made sure that Jews of many religious tendencies would feel at home in his organization, including those with no formal religious orientation.[37]

In approaching young people, the rabbis understood, as Lelyveld put it, that values couldn't be swallowed down, "like vitamins." They were the product of complex social relations. Learning them required practice, not abstract teaching.[38]

As the three men discussed the problem of creating the living conditions for a new generation of Jews to practice the social justice gospel of prophetic Judaism, they were both delighted and disturbed to see a successful, functioning organizational embodiment of their views. For over 15 years summer work camps had been established where visionary young men and women labored in righteousness against social inequity. Among the volunteers were many young Jewish idealists. The problem was that the camps, non-sectarian in their make-up, were organized by the American Friends Service Committee.

By 1949 the good works of the A.F.S.C. was the focus of international acclaim. The American group shared the 1947 Nobel Peace Prize with its British counterpart, the Friends Service Council of London. The prize came on the thirtieth anniversary of the American organization's birth, but the A.F.S.C. was rooted in a social tradition as old as the Friends' very existence.

The founder of the Friends was George Fox, born in Leicestershire in 1624 into the tumultuous revolutionary period that saw Puritan revolution against the monarchy and then grudging coexistence with the crown after the restoration. From the first, Fox's theology set himself and his followers apart from the harshness and exclusivity of the Puritan majority. Unconcerned with textural correctness, Fox sought to have his religion embody the spirit of the Sermon on the Mount:

> Blessed are the poor in spirit: for theirs is the kingdom of heaven.
> Blessed are they that mourn: for they shall be comforted.
> Blessed are the meek: for they shall inherit the earth.
> Blessed are they which do hunger and thirst after righteousness: for they shall be filled.
> Blessed are the merciful: for they shall obtain mercy.
> Blessed are the pure in heart: for they shall see God.
> Blessed are the peacemakers: for they shall be called the children of God.
> Blessed are they which are persecuted for righteousness' sake: for theirs is the kingdom of heaven.[39]

In its emphasis on appealing to the poor and disinherited, the Sermon on the Mount reflects the prophetic tradition; indeed in the next verse, Jesus mentions the persecution of the prophets and soon claims to be on earth to "fulfill" their teachings. In the twentieth century, Ferdinand Isserman had seen Jesus as the last of the biblical prophets while denying his status as God. Jesus was a political savior, a Jewish patriot "regarded by the masses of Jerusalem as their champion against the oppression of Rome...What Jew has not been critical of his brethren? What great Jew has not found flaws in Israel?" Moses and the prophets did.[40]

For Fox, feeling the spirit meant living a righteous life. Advocating an end to the hierarchical construction of the British church, Fox substituted monthly and yearly meetings. No man would have a title; each was to be addressed as

"Friend." Decisions would not be made by majority vote; that approach created winners and losers. Instead, meetings would continue discussion until a consensus was found. Worldly ambitions would be ignored, replaced instead by the higher motivations of ideal family life. As historian Howard Brinton expresses this notion:

> The family... is a small group which can be a valuable training ground for right behavior in a larger community. The members of a normal family cooperate with one another and share equally the family resources, the weak being entitled to receive what they require on the same terms as the strong. The food placed on the table is distributed according to need, not power to seize it.[41]

While alternately tolerated and persecuted in Britain, Fox's following was uniformly mistreated in the Massachusetts Bay Colony, where they were subject to frequent jailing, beatings, and torture. Their books were burned. In 1657 two Quakers were arrested for speaking in public in Salem; they were jailed for nine weeks in Boston, often denied food and water, and flogged with a three tailed whip 350 times each. It was a crime to bring a Quaker into the colony. Once deported, a Quaker who returned was to have his ear cut off; another attempt at re-entry would be punished with a tongue pierced by a hot iron. Two Friends did in fact lose ears.[42]

The Friends aroused the ire of the Puritans for many reasons but perhaps, as Brinton notes, "No Quaker belief aroused more opposition than the doctrine that the Light of Christ has been given to all men everywhere, since the beginning of the human race. This concept was particularly repugnant to those Protestants who believed that only the elect would be saved."[43]

Quakers practiced this theology by attempting to relate to the indigenous North Americans in Rhode Island and Pennsylvania as Friends, not conquerors. In Rhode Island, Indians were represented in all court cases involving them; no capital trial against an Indian could proceed unless the jury was 50% native. William Penn was determined that the land bearing his name would not be marked by violent clashes with the native people there. His Great Treaty of Friendship with the Leni-Lenape tribe in 1682, according to historian Gerald Jonas, legalized a "mutual understanding... erected by the Quaker colony of Pennsylvania, which for the next seventy-five years enjoyed virtual immunity from the Indian wars that periodically ravaged the other European settlements in North America."[44]

The most public voice of American Friends in the 18th century was John Woolman, born in New Jersey in 1720. Woolman, as Jonas notes, most often used the Old Testament prophets as the basis of his rhetoric.

> The rising up of a desire to obtain wealth is the beginning; this desire being cherished, moves to action; and riches thus gotten please self; and while self has a life in them it desires to have them defended. Wealth is attended by Power, by which bargains and proceedings contrary to Universal Righteousness are supported... May

we look upon our treasures, the furniture of our houses, and our garments, and try whether the seeds of war have nourishment in these our possessions[45]

Anti-slavery agitation came naturally to the Quakers as well, who were the first to publicly condemn the institution in 1688. By 1776 everyone in the faith renounced slavery; from then until emancipation, Quakers were best known in the United States for this intense opposition and the use of their homes as "stations" for the Underground Railroad. Friends Thomas Garrett and Levi Coffin each helped more than 3000 slaves escape.[46]

The Friends acted, as Jonas says, "on the belief that each human being represents an absolute value which must not be ignored, degraded, or exploited; along with this article of faith comes the acceptance of nonviolence as *a way of life*, and not just as a temporary tactic in a particular historical situation."[47]

This devotion to non-violence became pacifism for many Quakers. When Congress enacted draft legislation for World War I, a creative alternative was sought. The American Friends Service Committee was the solution. This would be the model for Isidor Hoffman's approach during World War II. Young men, be they Friends or of any faith, would have clear alternative service available to them. The A.F.S.C. would sponsor programs in Europe, close to the conflict, by which non-violent Americans would practice their opposition to armed conflict in a way that did not interfere with the stated aims of the American government. An assortment of American Progressive intellectuals and activists rallied to the A.F.S.C. cause. While the war raged, Conscientious Objectors under A.F.S.C. organizational leadership provided emergency medical assistance and organized to feed the hungry. At Verdun, site of one of the most horrific battlegrounds of the war, the group planted 25,000 trees.

Once the war ended, the massive needs of prostrate Europe dictated a continuing A.F.S.C. presence. From 1920 to 1924, the organization fed a million children a day in Germany, provided medical care and food for civil war torn revolutionary Russia, and replanted growing fields and fought typhus in Poland.

Inevitably, the A.F.S.C drew volunteers who couldn't finance a trip to Europe or didn't have large enough blocks of time to spend abroad. Demands grew for American projects. In 1924, the Home Service and the Interracial Service Sections were established. The latter group mainly brought speakers of color to college campuses. The former would evolve into the Social-Industrial Section, which by the 1930s led to an A.F.S.C. invasion of the coal fields. In 563 communities and 41 counties of Pennsylvania, Ohio, West Virginia, Tennessee, and Kentucky 40,000 children were given a meal a day throughout 1932.[48]

Many of the idealistic students of the depression were drawn to A.F.S.C. projects. They could be of any faith or of no faith, but they were eager to establish their humanity in service to others. By 1934 the A.F.S.C. had established a summer work project for college student volunteers. There 56 campers, 42 men and 14 women, installed a water supply for a mining community in rural Pennsylvania. By the following summer there were four work projects in mine country. When the campers weren't working they organized educational evenings, inviting mine officials, union activists and individual miners to speak. In 1936 five college student projects were joined by two made up of high school aged volunteers. The ideology of the camps was old-fashioned Quaker humanism and depression-era awareness. As a 1937 recruiting pamphlet put it:

> This generation of students must face a world threatened by war, torn by class strife and thwarted by poverty in the midst of plenty. They can be defeated by the thought of entering such a world or they can be challenged by it to start, during their student days, the building of a better one... Laboring with one's hands makes it possible, as nothing else can, to understand realistically the problems of the working class. Class barriers tend to disappear in the fellowship of hard, physical labor. A new appreciation of the intrinsic value of human personality is born. Work camps are laboratories in which problems of human relations and basic motivations may be experienced.[49]

Physical labor was always an important component of the projects. In the 1930s, projects built a community pool, playgrounds, a gristmill, a "fish-rearing pool" in conjunction with a TVA program, and renovated school buildings. One eliminated an Ohio city dump and replaced it with a playground.[50]

Though slowed by the Second World War, at mid-century A.F.S.C. volunteer camps continued to place idealistic students of all faiths throughout the United States and the world in humanitarian efforts requiring physical labor. In 1951 24 camps were conducted worldwide, four of them in the United States.

That year in Pine Mountain, Kentucky, 17 campers worked to create a farm machinery shed in the Appalachian Mountains. Historian Marvin Weisbord has recorded the struggle of the one black volunteer to overcome segregation and racism while working for the A.F.S.C. If Rabbis Isserman, Lelyveld, and Hoffman were watching, however, they would have not failed to notice another element: About half of the volunteers were Jewish.[51]

Though applauding the efforts of the A.F.S.C, the rabbis were concerned that the Jewish young people attending would never see the tie between their idealistic activity and what for them was its essence: prophetic Judaism in the modern age. Surely camps based on the A.F.S.C. model but under Jewish aegis and featuring "Jewish content" could simultaneously make a contribution as the Friends had while demonstrating the spiritual essence of Judaism to volunteers.

While Hoffman, Isserman, and Lelyveld were dedicated to the creation of a new Jewish work camp experience and were prepared to offer intellectual and philosophic guidance, they could or would not commit themselves to the nuts and bolts of building an organization. For this task they tapped an unlikely source by calling on a Wall Street attorney named Henry Kohn.

But if Wall Street was an improbable location for righteousness, Kohn was an unusual attorney. Already immersed in Isserman's prophetic Judaism, Kohn was possessed of both a voracious intellectual appetite and a hunger for meaningful activity. Manifest from his days as a St. Louis school boy, these qualities had driven and been encouraged by his academic and vocational choices.

Abandoned by his father several years after his birth, young Henry grew up in a household with three adults, his mother and her brother and father. A proud and determined woman, Henry's mother, Hannah Lederer, insisted that neither her daughter nor her son should be ashamed or feel their lives to be constrained because she was divorced. She constantly encouraged her children to walk tall and seize the moment. Life was too precious to waste an instant. All opportunities must be fully explored. Perhaps this belief in the limitlessness of her children's horizons stemmed from her long -standing American roots. Unlike most American Jews who are rooted in the great eastern European immigration of 1880-1920, Henry is descended on both sides from several generations of native born Americans with forbears in Germany, Hungary, Bohemia and what is now the Czech Republic.

Henry's uncle Leo Lederer lived the credo, balancing a career as a life insurance salesman with passionate involvement in St. Louis amateur theater. Though St. Louis was in many ways a traditional southern city, Henry's older sister Ruth would be no idle southern belle. College educated, she was motivated for a career in education and social service, working as a student teacher at Hull House in Chicago before starting and directing a nursery school at the St. Louis YM-YWHA. She moved to New York and mixed marriage with a long career in the New York City public schools and tireless devotion to Jewish service organizations.

Though limited by financial circumstances – while Henry was still in primary school his father disappeared from St. Louis and changed his name to avoid paying child support, even though he had a comfortable income from a family grocery chain – Henry's mother insisted there be no constraints on education. She proved the point by having her children commute long distances to take advantage of the best public education available in the St. Louis area.

This emphasis on education produced results. An accomplished achiever in all academic subjects, Kohn was less successful with junior high school electronic and mechanical drawing courses. It was obvious that his was to be a life of the mind. At Soldan High School his grades placed him in the elite of the school, and he was drawn to extracurricular activities that honed his intellect. He and A. E. Hotchner were the two-man St. Louis debating champs and in a series of matches that took place throughout the state, they proved themselves to be the unofficial champions of Missouri. Henry also joined the chess club, like the debating team advised by his high school homeroom teacher, Edward J. Mathie. The relationship between young protégé and mentor – one of several with adult males the fatherless young man was drawn to – was further strengthened by Mathie's invitation for Kohn to spend his summers working on his farm in Wisconsin. Kohn continues to regard this as a vital formative experience. He "learned the value of manual labor" and the hard work attendant to agricultural and rural life.

During his high school years, Kohn attended confirmation classes at Temple Israel taught by Ferdinand Isserman. Drawn to Isserman's charismatic speaking ability and the moral power of his vision, Kohn saw his rabbi as a "regional prophet." The confirmation classes encouraged Jewish young men to follow the righteous paths of the biblical prophets. His Friday night sermons contained this philosophy and his forthright warnings about the evil of fascism abroad and racial segregation in St. Louis. His young student was impressed with the vision and the biblical scholarship and world travel which informed it.

Kohn's superior achievement produced a flurry of college acceptances – at Harvard, the University of Chicago, and Yale. The latter school responded earliest and with an offer of a full academic scholarship. In the fall of 1935, the ambitious Missourian arrived in New Haven. Other young achievers enrolling that fall were William P. Bundy, William W. Scranton and Cyrus R. Vance.

Henry Kohn's days at Yale are a textbook model of what one's college experience should be. He plunged ahead into academic studies, where his main interest was in the social sciences, no great surprise for a socially concerned youngster during the days of the great depression. Avidly pursuing his courses, he was attracted to intellectual discussion wherever it took place, especially as a member of the Yale debating team. His only frustration lay in the limits of time. If five lectures were being offered on a given evening, it was clear he would only be able to hear two. Nor was he satisfied by what was offered. He became President of the Kohut Forum, a Jewish discussion group which preceded the arrival of Hillel at Yale.

Before long he began to explore his future professional career. Rabbi Maurice Zigmund, counselor to Yale's Jewish population, was so impressed with the student leader that he suggested a career as a rabbi. On his next trip to St. Louis, Kohn sought out Rabbi Isserman's advice; they agreed that the young man's ignorance of Hebrew would create stumbling blocks. After helping research a professor's book on economics, Henry was encouraged to get a doctorate in that field. But law appealed more, because it offered varied opportunities for both intellectual expression and the resolution of conflict where a young man might further sharpen his wits.

Once again both Harvard and Yale accepted him; now he had more reason for staying at Yale. Again he seized learning opportunities in and out of the classroom. He would graduate in the top 10% of the law school class; he would write and edit articles in the Yale Law Journal, including a lengthy piece on wartime price controls; he would again attend lectures by the vast array of worldly scholars appearing on the campus. Among the most influential of these during Kohn's undergraduate and law school days was Reinhold Niebuhr. Niebuhr's meditations on grace and sin were powerfully connected to his compassion for the depression's victims. A pessimist about capitalism and socialism, Niebuhr nonetheless forcefully argued that Christianity demanded protection for society's underclass. Here was a renowned Christian theologian echoing themes of the prophetic Judaism of Ferdinand Isserman. (For Henry Kohn, this is no coincidence. Neibuhr's Lutheran church has its theologic center in St. Louis; Kohn sees a cross-fertilization between Jewish and Lutheran religious and social thought.)

The bombing of Pearl Harbor accelerated everyone's schooling. Henry Kohn graduated from Yale Law School in February 1942 and was hired by the Board of Economic Warfare to help administer the very price controls he had dissected in the Law Journal. His job soon evolved into helping to secure war materials for America's allies and denying them to the Axis powers. He had the job only until he was drafted; after basic training he was enrolled in Officer's Candidate School, and soon he was working at the Pentagon, helping to supervise the huge army post exchange system.

Stationed at the Blackstone Hotel in New York, he met and fell in love with Anne Frankenthaler. Though intending to return to St. Louis after their marriage in September 1945 to begin a law practice there, he acceded to her request to remain in New York and join her father's firm.

George Frankenthaler was the last of the great mentors in Henry Kohn's life. A man of legendary honesty, Frankenthaler had developed a successful surrogate's practice. He invited his son-in-law to join the firm, encouraging him to expand its borders. The timing was propitious. Frankenthaler was elected Surrogate of New York County in 1948. While the Judge served the public's will, Henry could maintain the firm's clients while striking out in whatever direction pleased him. Looking back fifty years later, Kohn wrote that, "The practice of the firm has been of a general character, excluding criminal law and negligence, but including some litigation, nurturing of new businesses, especially venture capital, representing corporations from their inception, as well as established ones... By and large the idea of taking on a matter which was new and different didn't phase me." Drawing confidence from his excellent achievement at Yale, Kohn plunged ahead. Though he generally tried to keep his clients out of the courts, Kohn successfully sued both 3M and New York Telephone, enjoying researching the legal precedents to trim the sails of his mighty opponents.

Deeply immersed in his law firm and with raising his young family – Margaret was born in 1948, Barbara in 1950, and Alice would follow in 1952 – Kohn was contacted by Ferdinand Isserman and his colleagues in the fall of 1949 with another "matter that was new and different."

"Henry," said Isserman, "How about organizing a Jewish work camp patterned after the Friends' work camp program?" At the initial meeting he made clear that he would not accept Isidor Hoffman's pacifism or Arthur Lelyveld's celebrated Zionism as guidelines. Kohn had encountered militant pacifism while at Yale; he engaged in long debates with young Dave Dellinger about draft resistance.

At a 1939 speech before the Yale Political Union he confronted the peace faction with the dire consequences of failing to confront Nazi Germany with military force. The campus had been a hotbed of pacifist activity; Yale, Kohn remembers, "probably had the largest number – per capita – of conscientious objectors in jail during the war." Kohn heard pleas for non-cooperation with selective service; he emphatically rejected them. He wrote a piece for the Yale Literary Magazine entitled "The Fetish of the Open Mind" deriding the pacifist position. For him it was axiomatic that Hitlerism must be defeated by military means.

Nor was he sure that Zionism was necessarily the post-war direction for American Jewry. In the late 1940s, while most – though not all – Jews in the United States supported the creation of Israel, many insisted that American life held the best promise for its Jewish citizens.

The rabbis themselves were political militants; the attorney was not. While Isserman and Hoffman embraced the dissident Jeremiads of their biblical inspiration, Kohn interpreted prophetic Judaism as a humanitarian impulse that might unify people of many viewpoints. Pointedly he told the rabbis that if they wanted pacifism or Zionism he was not their man.

Given that "I was only game in town," Hoffman retreated to an insistence on "Jewish content." Now Kohn responded positively, for he revered Isserman, and here was an opportunity to pursue his Judaism with the same devotion and energy he lavished on his academic and professional career.[52] The problem now was: How to make it work?

2

Chapter Two: Origins and Early Struggles

Having made the commitment to form a young people's Jewish service organization, Henry Kohn faced his limitations. He had no experience in camping and, outside of his working summer vacations on his debate coach's farm, no experience with manual labor. Though only seven years removed from the college campus, he had no particular knowledge of working with young people. He had no resources for recruiting volunteers, hiring camp supervisory personnel, or selecting work projects.

What he did have was a prodigious intellect, youthful self-confidence, loquacious persuasiveness, and a collection of like-minded and similarly situated friends, aspiring Jewish professionals and business people. Shortly after committing his own effort to the three rabbis, Kohn called a meeting in his Manhattan apartment of his interested friends to begin looking into the possibilities of forming a group.

One early exercise was researching the activities of existing Jewish organizations to make sure the work was not already being accomplished. A survey of some 120 Jewish service organizations found all of them to be inwardly directed. Though some, like the Henry Street Settlement House or the Anti-Defamation League, had easily broadened their concerns from defense of Jews in need to support of others in similar situations, no organization was entirely focussed on the needs of the outside world. Given the historic legacy of anti-Semitism and Peter Stuyvesant's warning to the initial Jewish immigrants to New Amsterdam – "Take care of your own" – this focus had not been surprising. The new psychological impact of the establishment of Israel, which literally "put Jews on the map," made an outwardly directed Jewish organization possible. The state's survival was a sign that Jews had arrived enough to take the risk of caring for others.

Initially, the association focussed on trying to raise seed money to make the project possible. Several estimates were offered, but the collection of friendly amateurs decided that an initial kitty of $25,000 would be necessary to hire an executive director, rent an office and supply the first project with operating funds. Taxing each interested family $10.00, individuals sought support from established charities, Jew and Gentile. The work was without reward, financial or psychological, as the kitty refused to grow into a grown cat. Jewish charity organizations were uninterested; Gentile ones could hardly be expected to see the need for a Jewish young people's service organization.

Finally, in the fall of 1950, Bernice Wallace suggested that if the group waited for enough money to establish a functioning office, it might be waiting forever. Perhaps the way to establish the organization was to run a pilot project with no paid New York staff by making use of the limited resources available to the group. Office and other organizational needs would be supplied without reimbursement by those assembled in Henry Kohn's apartment. Practically this would mean that Kohn's law office would handle the clerical work, Kohn himself would handle most of the administrative duties, and his coterie of interested friends would become his sounding board. Soon the most interested of these friends would be called the Board of Directors. Rabbis Hoffman, Isserman, and Lelyveld's names would appear as board members, too, from the first listing until each man's death, but only Hoffman would take an active role. Perhaps it was for reasons of geography (Hoffman was at Columbia University in Manhattan, while Isserman and Lelyveld were situated in St. Louis and Cleveland), or perhaps it was because Hoffman's daily activities brought him into contact with college students, but only the conservative rabbi became a vital and active molder of the infant organization, working alongside a lay group whose members were mostly reform in religious orientation.

To offset the collective inexperience, the nascent board of directors looked for guidance from the New York office of the American Friends Service Committee. Hoffman had contacts there; by November 1950, AFSC area director Sanford Kravitz had become an active member of the Jewish organization's board. Initially, his help was to prove vital.[1]

He sent Kohn a lengthy internal evaluation of "AFSC U.S. Work Camps, Summer 1950" which examined policy issues facing the Friends, and by extension, the new organization as well. Every issue confronted by the AFSC would be fodder for the eager Manhattanites meeting in Henry Kohn's apartment to chew on. Were the sites "the types of communities... and the projects on which we work of the kind where work camps can make the greatest contribution?" Were the project sponsors "well enough planned and coordinated" before and during the summer? Was the leadership of the work project, including a dietician, able enough? Did the campers represent a "variety" of volunteers? On the most obvious level, this should be less of an issue in the new organization, where presumably the volunteers would mostly be Jewish. However, there were many kinds of Jews: How much of a variety would be helpful? The AFSC document pondered improving educational opportunities at the site. It also raised contentious issues in any camping situation: "sleep, coupling, KP, leisure time."[2]

As the evaluation pamphlet continued, it was obvious that even an experienced organization with many resources confronted problems. Several projects had failed to provide meaningful work; others were faulted for poor interaction with the surrounding communities or lack of meaningful educational opportunities. Sometimes the sponsors had failed to meet their obligations for reasons both beyond and within their control.

One salient fact must have caught the eye of Hoffman, Kohn and the others: of the 62 senior (college age) AFSC volunteers who listed religious affiliation in 1950, nine were Jews; in the junior (high school age) volunteers 15 of 51 noting religion were Jewish. By far the largest single religious denomination at AFSC work camps in 1950 were Jews. There was no way of knowing how many of the 36 who were listed as "unknown" or "none" came from Jewish families.

One unequivocal finding of the pamphlet was endorsed by the new board: Campers desired and approved strong leadership at the project site.

In January 1951 the Board of Directors was formally selected; the organization still had no name, no place to send volunteers, no volunteers to send, and no project director. By February Kravitz had researched and selected a few past AFSC work camps as potential candidates for the pilot project. He guessed the whole cost of a full project – 16 volunteers, a director and a dietician – would be under $6,000.

In April a spirited discussion about the group's name was concluded. American Jewish Service Committee seemed an obvious choice, but the directors were concerned that the organization not seem an adjunct to or simply a pale copy of the Friends. American Jewish Society for Service was a linguistic tribute to the AFSC while still suggesting independence.

Should the group be coeducational? The AFSC projects were; still, the matter was not decided until the spring. Could the girls handle the labor? Subsequent history was to prove that girls were more eager to volunteer and did every bit as much work as the boys, but Rosie the Riveter was already becoming a forgotten icon in 1951 as females faded into a last decade of apparently compliant domesticity. Nonetheless, after consideration, AJSS decided to emulate AFSC practice and recruit from both sexes.

Finally, what age group would be recruited? Two factors encouraged the "senior" camp approach. Board members thought college age volunteers would be more mature and work harder than high school age equivalents. Furthermore, for the adults with no recruiting experience, college students seemed easier targets. After all, Rabbi Lelyveld was national director of Hillel, the Jewish campus organization, and Rabbi Hoffman's leadership of Jewish students at Columbia and his network of contacts at other campuses were the only known sources of volunteers.

Hillel campus directors did respond to a directive from Lelyveld, but the recruiting results were unexpectedly meager. Kohn thought campus Hillel directors were overworked, but perhaps those Jewish students most eager to participate in service directed to the outer world were not prone to be in Jewish organizations, where the prophetic message was a less likely focus than providing an institutional framework for maintaining family traditions away from home or expressing support for Israel. Large numbers of Jewish young people were interested in outreach to others; it is arguable whether Hillel was the place to find them.

Certainly, in the spring of 1951 the AJSS did not locate substantial numbers. Twenty prospective volunteers expressed a measure of commitment, but by July 3, when the project began, only six volunteers were enrolled. Fifteen potential campers went elsewhere; at least one chose an AFSC project instead. For that young woman, having "Jewish content" was not a significant factor in selecting a summer of service. Perhaps the AFSC's established reputation was more relevant.

The AFSC connection proved significant in selecting the first AJSS project directors. Irwin Stark's resume showed impressive academic credentials. An English teacher in the New York City public schools, he was the author of several published short stories, poetry and a novel, released in 1948. His wife Alice had a history of working with non-profit organizations. She was active in the pacifist Fellowship of Reconciliation and had worked under A. Philip Randolph as a secretary to the National Committee for a Permanent FEPC (a wartime Roosevelt government agency aimed at eliminating race discrimination in hiring practices, particularly with firms doing business with the federal government). She had attended an AFSC work camp as a teenager, and in 1939 she and her husband had toured AFSC work camps throughout the country.

The couple seemed ideal. Committed Jewish intellectuals, they had been interested enough in the Quaker approach to have spent a summer investigating its operation. Surely, they would provide precisely the mature leadership the fledgling group needed to launch its first flight.

Alice Stark had no official role. In the early years, the male partner was identified as the director or project leader. It would take the appearance of the feminist movement and some emphatic insistence by "directors' wives" to abolish the archaic reference to "director and wife" and to recognize that if a couple was being hired, it was to be assumed they would be sharing the responsibilities of leadership. That recognition was still 23 years in the future when the Starks were welcomed by the AJSS board.[3]

They would be heading out to Indianapolis, Indiana, to work for Flanner House, an independent organization dedicated to providing decent housing for black war veterans. The American Friends Service Committee had sent a work project there in 1946.[4]

The post-war housing shortage made newspaper headlines throughout American metropolitan areas. The war had brought change and renewed population expansion to the cities after the stagnation and decrepitude of the long depression period; like most domestic matters during World War II, housing was a "back burner" issue which only began to heat up after the world-wide conflagration was successfully extinguished. Now working and middle class Americans sought new dwellings to replace older, cramped, and antiquated apartments, with more modern plumbing and electrical facilities. Even as an increasingly conservative Congress retreated from the New Deal's social agenda, the Truman administration recognized the gravity of the housing shortage. The Housing Act of 1949 enabled the construction of over 800,000 low income units, funded slum removal, and provided federal mortgage help for the middle class.[5]

For black Americans in the big cities, housing was indeed a crisis issue. The early part of the century had seen a massive internal migration of south to north; mechanization of the cotton fields, World War I, the lure of the new assembly line jobs (to which few African Americans were given access) depression, and World War II each accelerated the drive northward.[6] After the Second World War and black Americans' combat experience in the still segregated army, return to the Jim Crow south seemed all the more intolerable. The exodus northward continued.

There was little guarantee that freer access to jobs, education, and housing would be available to the new arrivals. In many of the cities of the mid-west the same forces which had driven southern blacks away had spurred movements of poorer whites northward. They were unlikely to leave racism behind; nor were northerners necessarily prepared to open their arms to their former slave "brothers." De facto limits on job opportunities and strictly enforced (if not codified by law) geographical boundaries often limited black Americans to the poorest pockets of the expanding cities.

Indianapolis was no exception. In the immediate post-war period, it was the northern city with the greatest percentage of African-American residents. The racial divide was maintained in part by the open marching of the Ku Klux Klan through its main streets. Irwin Stark wrote in early 1952 that the city's "slums are worse than those of Chicago, Memphis, Birmingham or Washington," and he quoted a contemporary architectural journal's more graphic description of a city of

> streets and streets of hovels, the streets often only muddy paths. Many of these hovels have no toilets and no running water. A group of families patronizes a community privy and a community pump. Beyond the slum is a vast dump heap, ragged gravel pits and then a stream... One shack with an assessed valuation of $850, which would seem an exaggeration, rents for $35 a month. Nearby is a coal shed rented to a family for $7 a month. It even has a street number and there is a service flag in the window.[7]

The city attempted to redress some of these grievances by purchasing acreage under eminent domain legislation in 1945. Local settlement house director Cleo Blackburn, appealing to city financial interests, organized in opposition to real estate barons who sought to frustrate slum removal. Flanner House was established as a sweat equity project for black veterans with stable financial backgrounds. By the time the AJSS arrived in 1951, 21 families were at work building their own homes.[8]

The tiny AJSS pilot group moved into the Indiana State Federation of Colored Women's Clubs which enabled volunteers to walk to work after spending their nights on army cots borrowed from the local Red Cross. Proving the old adage that if a town had two Jews, it would also have three synagogues,[9] the small collection managed to represent a cross-section of the American Jewish experience. Two of the volunteers were Orthodox and scholarly, seeking advanced degrees in prestigious universities; one was Reform with only the most limited ritual involvement in Judaism; two were atheists, one actively hostile to organized religion of any sort; one was not Jewish at all. His "background was nominal Protestantism. I had attended Presbyterian churches as a child and had recently switched to a Methodist church for purely social reasons. Practically I was a humanist. In any case, I was accepted by AJSS. My parents were not exactly overjoyed but were fairly liberal and let me do what I wanted to do."[10] He had been recommended to the AJSS by the AFSC when the latter had no space available on its projects. The Starks themselves were Reform Jews with an appreciation for both prophetic Judaism and active social awareness.

The motives of the group members were complex. One of the volunteers had signed on because he was an aspiring filmmaker who wanted to shoot a super-8 movie of the project. At 29 he was an unusually old "camper." The Kentucky volunteer, Paul Doudna, who at 19 was the youngest of the group, "had always been handy with tools so the prospect of working on housing was appealing on those grounds alone."[11] Though not particularly articulate, all were drawn to service in part from humanitarian impulses.

The AJSS, of course, had been founded to direct this humanism into meaningful activity, theoretically grounded in prophetic Judaism. The Starks, therefore, had several assignments. They had to make sure that the Flanner House organization provided the volunteers with suitable work and that everyone participated meaningfully in the labor. They had to locate religious and educational services in the city, which would foster general learning and spiritual guidance. They had to construct a religious program to provide the theoretical basis for the activity itself. All of this was to be done in as democratic a way as possible, so that the volunteers genuinely felt that they were creating their own summer.

From the first summer, Rabbi Hoffman took a leading role in organizing religious study. In personal meetings with the Starks and in letters to them before the summer began and in a long weekend spent in Indianapolis, Hoffman proposed several particulars to give shape to the vaguely described "Jewish content" to which the new organization was committed. Hoffman would continue to brief project directors on shaping the religious component of AJSS summers into the 1970s.

Friday evenings were devoted to a group observance. The group ate challah, recited the traditional prayers over the bread, and lit the candles to usher in the Sabbath.

This became a source of dispute with Dan Berman, the "vehement anti-ritualist" as Irwin Stark described him. He did not want to observe the Sabbath, but when Paul Doudna reminded him that he had the right to not attend (as the organization evolved, abstention from Friday night services – or any group activity – would not be an option), he decided to stay, though he was often sullen.

On Saturday mornings the group attended religious services in Indianapolis. This was almost a complete fiasco, as "the nearby Reform congregation, where the presence of the campers one Saturday morning just about made a *minyan*, proved a disappointment even for those who had habitually attended Reform services at home. The absence of the regular rabbi, who was on vacation, seemed an insufficient excuse for the drab and perfunctory worship which they witnessed. Without singing, without feeling, without worshipers, it proved a depressing and embarrassing occasion."[12]

After experimenting with other congregations, the contingent found it was happiest in the Orthodox synagogue, where they were welcomed enthusiastically and invited to read from the Torah. This would prove an unusual occurrence, as unique as the presence of Orthodox campers in the group.

Once a week Milton Steinberg's *Basic Judaism* was used as a text for discussion within the crew. Steinberg's book, a common sense conservative explanation of Jewish ritual, made no one particularly happy, as it was denounced by both the Orthodox and the non-religious members of the assemblage. When one of the Orthodox campers substituted a reading from his own ritual, a lively discussion ensued, much to the surprise of the Starks.

Finally, at Hoffman's insistence, the group institutionalized the Quaker camp practice of meditation. Again both the Orthodox and secular Jews revolted; the ritual was tolerated rather than practiced, and Dan Berman had to be reprimanded for talking and smoking during meditation. The religious aspect could not be considered a success.

Education, on the other hand, was impressive. Formal speakers included Flanner House President Cleo Blackburn, an organizer for the United Steel Workers, two social workers, a vice-president of a department store, a representative of the Federal Housing Project, an economics professor, and the president of a coal cooperative. The speakers were challenged by politically outspoken campers.

By far the greatest educational experience was provided by living and working in the black community. As campers worked alongside people they would have been unlikely to know, they learned first hand how northern racism and poverty affected the lives of those they came to help. They were profusely thanked by Flanner House residents and neighbors and were awarded heroic tribute in the black press. (All of the local papers covered the project and the *National Jewish Post*, published in Indianapolis, made the 1951 summer project the focus of several feature stories.[13])

The Flanner House organization's invitation to the AJSS aimed at two objectives: additional labor and the "seasoning" of the veterans by creating a positive social interaction with outsiders. Both objectives were satisfied, though clearly the small numbers of the AJSS contingent accomplished less than what might have been anticipated. Still, the group gave 750 hours of work and helped to create nearly two finished homes. The Starks noted that the

> Work was varied. We shingled roofs (5 of them) nailed flooring, roofing and siding, hauled Indiana limestone (one of the campers [Paul Doudna] became a stone cutter), tamped basements, helped lay cement for the flooring of foundations and for basements, painted, loaded and unloaded sheetrock, helped set up the prefabricated walls of houses, dug ditches, unloaded a lumber freight car, helped set in I-beams and prepared cement block for the masons. We also cleaned up around the project and did numerous other chores of an unskilled nature.[14]

Most of the campers worked well, though the aspiring filmmaker seemed both less capable and less committed than the others. Doudna, the young Methodist with construction experience, was both most adept and most willing.

The work provided almost everyone with "a deeply gratifying experience... While only one of our group developed any special skill, the rest of us learned how to use shovel, hammer, and pick and gained a good deal of common sense in the performance of manual labor."[15]

There was social tension in the small contingent. Berman objected to more than religion. He explained that he had signed on for the work aspect of the program and did not feel compelled to attend other events. He complained that the food was unappetizing and insufficient. A glance at the menus makes the reader incredulous. All three daily meals seem filling and balanced from the 1950s' stress on protein, starch and vegetable. Breakfast invariably included hot and cold dishes, lunches were hearty and dinner included several courses and dessert.

No great social ties were formed in the group despite a general sense of satisfaction with what had been accomplished.

Overall satisfaction was felt by Kohn, Hoffman and the rest of the Board of Directors. The work had been good, the interaction with the biblical "stranger" excellent, and the development of a civic ideal tied to Judaism had been accomplished. Though problems remained with recruiting, religious programming, and creating a positive social environment, the new organization had made a successful beginning.

The Starks made many recommendations for the future. A preliminary trip by the project director to see the site and meet with project hosts and those providing support services seemed vital, as did an orientation meeting in advance to stress the need for cooperative living. The group should have vehicular transportation available to facilitate recreation and education. The Board adopted all of these recommendations. The Starks also proposed screening procedures to discourage those whose purposes seemed antithetical to AJSS tenets. But given the struggle with recruitment, this would be more difficult to accomplish.

Indeed, recruiting for 1952 provided as small a collection for the second project as the first. Despite the efforts of Hillel college counselors and an impressive personal effort by Isidor Hoffman's son Dan, who indefatigably blitzed upper New York and lower New England campuses on a two week speaking tour for the AJSS, only six volunteers, paying $10 each for the privilege, signed on. Dan Hoffman's speeches attracted dozens of "interested" listeners at each campus - attendance rosters from these events often contain as many as 50 names – but follow-up phone calls and letters produced no results. Another feature of 1951 was unfortunately repeated: 16 had signed on as prospective campers; as the summer approached, 11 withdrew. As in the previous summer, the volunteers were a heterogeneous contingent. Their ages ranged between 20 and 30.

The campers would be working with new directors, Hyman and Nora Sankel. Irwin Stark made the transition from public school to academic teaching (he was appointed to the English Department of the City College of New York), and the Starks did not reapply.

Hyman Sankel had varied experiences working with young people. A former camp director and teacher, he was a New York City high school principal who taught Hebrew School in Manhattan and had run the youth services program at his own temple in Queens.

Again, the AJSS group would be working for the most needy of Americans, but this time it would be removed from the big city, though the population being served was certainly urban. The project host was the Morningside Community Center of west Harlem. The institution being served was the creation of its director, Jarrett Robinson, who had founded Forest Lake Camp in Rabbit Hollow, New Hampshire as a place for underprivileged city youngsters to experience the country. For the second time, the services provided by AJSS volunteers would benefit black Americans, still the most despised and least empowered of American citizens. Once again, the AJSS chose a site previously visited by the AFSC.

Jarrett Robinson was a pioneer in advancing race relations. Like his namesake Jackie, he had dared to introduce African Americans where virtually none had gone before. When he opened his camps (one for boys and one for girls) there had been grumbling about the unsuitabilty of his clients for rural New England, but by the early 1950s the camp was a great success. 780 kids were served in 1951; local opposition had dried up. Hy Sankel noted, "It took courage, stamina, and intelligence to establish an interracial camp outside of Winchester, New Hampshire."

The AJSS volunteers were given a variety of tasks. They built a supply house and replaced the girls' showers by installing seven new showerheads; they constructed a new outhouse with four seats that legally enabled 35 additional children to attend camp. They excavated for toilets, applied wood stain to the interior of the infirmary, built a platform for a water fountain and built shelves. On rainy days they served as counselors, supervising games and substituting in the dining hall for counselors on their days off. When the AJSS project ended, two of the girls remained at Forest Lake as counselors. For such a small contingent their work record was impressive.

Religion was once again a subject for contention. Many of the volunteers were indifferent to Jewish ritual; Steinberg's book and meditation were again resisted by some. The campers preferred sleeping late to creating Saturday morning services; two Protestant campers attended, but the two Jewish girls did not. Once again the nearby congregation was on vacation.

There was conflict between the sexes as the young men resented the females' desire to include Forest Lake male counselors on recreation outings. In a rural setting, transportation provided by Forest Lake enabled the AJSS volunteers to visit Tanglewood, climb Mt. Monadnock, visit the Cathedral in the Pines, take a seven mile hike and attend a local folk dance. Education evenings included visits by three rabbis including Hoffman and talks by Dr. Robinson and a representative of the New England Friends Service Committee.

Feedback from the campers indicated that they felt they were too old to be supervised. The Sankels were considered heavy-handed by a few who wrote to Henry Kohn in the fall. Requests by some to leave the group on weekends were turned down. The mature ages of the volunteers made it difficult to impose rules; when the Sankels attempted this, they were often considered dictatorial. A young woman complained that Hy Sankel wanted to apply "grade school" discipline to college students. One of the campers thought the group was "too heterogeneous . . . ages, personalities and interests of the campers were too varied." Another resented having to "run around" on weekends. One of the group left early, though her letter glowed with only positive responses. More than one felt the emphasis on Jewish religious content was an intrusion.

1952 was the last summer that the project would be dominated by college students. Originally it was thought that they would be easier to recruit and more likely to take a mature outlook toward the work, but college age volunteers had been scarce indeed. Only twelve had worked over the first two summers – and several were past normal college age. The "maturity" of the campers had actually led to some difficulties. They had signed on to work, but did not necessarily buy into planned evening and weekend activities. Several had expressed feisty hostility to any non-work programming; complaints about community living are featured in a few letters from the 1952 group.

The Board decided to experiment in 1953. The organization would return to Rabbit Hollow and the Sankels would once again direct, but this time with a high school contingent. Meanwhile, a final attempt would be made with college age volunteers. Another director, Rabbi Max Ticktin, would guide this contingent. When the summer was over, AJSS could compare the experiences and decide to continue with what the AFSC labeled "senior" or "junior" camps.

The only way to accomplish the comparison was to successfully recruit for the two groups. Henry Kohn addressed students at Yale and urged all board members to similarly solicit volunteers at their alma maters. Again Hillel and Dan Hoffman were put to work, but this time advertising and outreach to local temples and temple youth groups was initiated. By spring AJSS had discovered the power of the *New York Times Magazine*; its camp section was already established as the principal print message for east coast camping. Additional ads ran in other New York broadsheets and in synagogue newsletters. The resulting pay-off was 56 inquiries between late February and early June of 1953.

The result of this weighty campaign might have tipped the scales on the experiment before one hammer or paintbrush was lifted. AJSS would send 13 high school age youngsters to New Hampshire in 1953; five college age volunteers would be headed up to the Hawthorne Cedar Knolls school for emotionally disturbed youngsters in Westchester, New York, operated by the Jewish Board of Guardians.

Why had college recruiting proved so disappointing? As previously mentioned, the most outer directed Jews on the campus might not necessarily have been found in Hillel or other Jewish organizations. Signing on to a Quaker sponsored work camp might have appeared more attractive for the very reason that the organization was exotic; its storied legacy of the underground railroad and pacifist alternative service was new and therefore inherently fascinating for its volunteers. Going away to college means loosening ties to family. Those eager to make their own mark on the world might have perceived AJSS – if they ever heard of it, of course – as binding them to their parents' way.

In addition, AJSS conceived of the summer as far more than the work camp experience. To include work, "Jewish content," education and a full investigation of the local area into one summer necessarily mandated a round the clock, seven days a week schedule. The college students at the first two work camps were used to making more independent decisions – including decisions not to operate as a collective. The resentments expressed by Dan Berman in Indianapolis and by several campers in September 1952 letters to Henry Kohn were frequently rebellions against a full structuring of the experience.

It should come as little surprise, then, that the high school contingent enjoyed a much more successful summer than the small group working under the supervision of Rabbi Ticktin. At Hawthorne Cedar Knolls the five campers were given a choice of assignments. They "enthusiastically selected" painting a building which was slated to be used for a "pioneer experiment in intensive therapy for 'extremely disturbed' children." The tiny AJSS group was delighted to work on a building that would be used for the most needy. The work itself, however, was not exciting, as the repetitive nature of the task took its toll.

In the afternoon, each volunteer spent time as a personal counselor with a school child, and even the recreation choices were mostly those of the school itself. Ticktin's report shows exasperation with his charges, whom he faults for being ineffective in labor, unimaginative in recreation, and disinterested in Judaism. He and his wife, he claims, felt called upon to administer to a small cluster of the troubled, generalizing from his experience to conclude that AJSS

> will continue to attract a high percentage of non-conformist and even so-called neurotic persons. The challenge of a work camp is especially felt by the university student who has not allowed himself to be swallowed up by the more conformist mores of the campus and accordingly we will always have persons who are looking for resolution of personal problems in work camp activity or political and religious radicals.[18]

Even with this "understanding," Ticktin found two of the five to be disturbed beyond the limit of acceptability and called for better screening. He also recommended that the organization avoid institutional settings and suggested projects with more physically demanding labor: the harder the better.

The contrast with the Sankels' report could not have been greater. A group of 13 campers demolished a 100 year old barn and erected a new wing to the dining hall. The elimination of the barn proved a major boon to community relations between Rabbit Hollow and the surrounding community, since the building was not actually on the camp site but in the town of Winchester. Town residents had been too poor to remove a twenty year old eyesore and the local government refused to pay for a private misfortune. Thus, AJSS contributed to the continued easing of racial tensions between the predominately black camp and the 100% white surrounding community. The dining room addition, by contrast, was less enthusiastically received, as it turned out to be for the use of the cooks and not directly related to camper activity. One problem was the surprising gender breakdown. Only two of the thirteen volunteers were boys. (AJSS would prove to have a consistently easier time attracting the so-called weaker sex to its summers of physical labor.)

Four visiting rabbis, including Hoffman, made effective presentations, and several campers, three of whom were flirting with Unitarianism or Quaker beliefs, strengthened their commitment to their Jewish heritage. Several of the campers told the Sankels they wanted to return to AJSS for the following summer.[19] The campers produced their own mimeographed newsletter, "The Work Camper," which contains the reflections of nine volunteers. These are almost all thoughtful and positive, reflecting a unity and acceptance of group values absent in the college age contingents.

In the fall, the Board announced its intention to field two projects for campers ages 16-18 in 1954.[20]

Unfortunately there was a considerable difference between announcing and producing. Recruitment for the infant organization was slower than anticipated. Given the larger desire to conduct projects at all, the Board accepted volunteers of whatever ages in 1954 and 1955, each time staffed by small contingents. Ten volunteers from 16 to 23 years of age built an outdoor recreational center in a state park in the West Virginia mountains; a similar assemblage renovated a community center to ease tension between new suburbanites and rural folk in the second Levittown outside of Fallsington, Pennsylvania. By the following year, the AJSS only recruited nine volunteers; they engaged in various outdoor maintenance activities at the Highlander Folk School in Monteagle, Tennessee. With no network of non-profit organizations to locate potential projects, the AJSS continued to walk many of the paths blazed by earlier AFSC camps.

The difference in maturity, independence and malleability between campers of 16 and those of 23 continued to deny group cohesion in these early years. AJSS was in no position to turn down prospective volunteers, nor were there effective criteria to do so.

Several of the volunteers seemed to make Rabbi Ticktin look like a seer; the West Virginia group in particular seems to have been peopled with unhappy souls. Four of the boys were sent home; the group actually voted to ask two of them to leave. Director Rabbi Alexander Feinsilver characterized one camper as

> a sick boy who should have careful psychiatric care, as I told his mother before sending him home... Two of the boys had run away from home in the past; one misrepresented his age to the Society; another had spent time in an orphanage and more recently was living with step-mother and step-brothers.[21]

Nor was Feinsilver keen on his girl recruits, who, he claimed, "exhibited a striking lack of respect for anybody and anything... in the beginning 'I hate you' and 'Drop dead' were the two most frequent expressions." He concluded that of his volunteers, "only one boy and perhaps three or four of the girls were suited temperamentally and emotionally for such a serious undertaking."[22]

The lack of sympathy between director and campers was even more evident at the Highlander Folk School where Morton Kanter, newly married and fresh out of a Reform rabbinical school, found difficulty with his assignment. Abruptly he left the group in the care of boys counselor Everett Gendler, a closer protégé of conservative Rabbi Hoffman, and the supervising administrator of the host organization. The AJSS was fortunate to have Kohn's relationship of mutual trust with the Highlander leadership and a male counselor of such great personal responsibility to save the project.[23]

While there is some evidence that the heterogeneity of the campers was posing great difficulties, the consistent lack of sympathy between the three rabbis selected by Isidor Hoffman to pilot projects in 1953, 1954, and 1955 and the youth they were supposed to guide suggests that some of the problem lay with the leadership.

A course of study at rabbinical school might auger significant Jewish content, but it certainly did not guarantee understanding or empathy with young people. Since many of the volunteers were non-observant Jews, including a few each summer who were entirely secular, conflict about the meaning of "Jewish content" was inevitable. Though the left-wing tradition was beginning to fade with the dawning of the suburban age, many of the volunteers in the 1950s and 1960s were raised in the culture of *yiddishkeit* – the offspring of Jewish Zionist, socialist and communist movements for whom Judaism meant Israeli folk dances, Yiddish folk songs, and nostalgia for Jewish trade unionism and the Yiddish socialist press.[24] Such youngsters might be indifferent or hostile to attempts to engage them in traditional religious practice, but it did not mean that they would reject a commitment to the prophetic ideal. Young graduates of rabbinical school might not be able to be sympathetic with this heritage. Indeed, coming out of a scholarly tradition, many might adopt a didactic tone that would alienate their charges from the outset.

Nor was there any guarantee they would be sensitive to the social needs of young people. Rabbinical students are by definition more aware of religious inspiration and less attracted to the varied secular culture which influences many young people in high school and college.

Rabbi Hoffman had more success with finding a director who was attuned to the feelings of his charges with Hillel leader Don Michaelson, who directed the second 1954 summer project in Pennsylvania. The work on the community center was well organized, and Michaelson proved to be a sympathetic listener to the concerns of his young charges.

But Michaelson, like the rabbis, made only a commitment for a single summer. Thus, the opportunity to learn from one's own past experiences – probably the most important single characteristic in developing leadership skills – was absent in the first several summers.

The American Friends Service Committee was also exploring the difficulties of attracting receptive leadership. In 1953 the AFSC published a handbook for project leaders which stressed a committee system to guide the working of the camps and established philosophic guidelines for what made an effective project director. He "should do his share of labor," "be able to mix freely" with kids, host visitors – but not too many, and "be more mature than the campers, having thought more deeply into his philosophy of life and achieved a greater degree of emotional stability, security and calmness." He should lead

> discussions to take initiatives in planning camp activities without being too dictatorial. . . Last, but perhaps most important, the director must be motivated by a deep religious conviction of the worth of human personality and not merely theological knowledge of god. A

loving, spirit and a genuine sympathy with the campers is necessary for camp to be "a harmonious, creative society." [25]

Henry Kohn and the Board were slowly learning this lesson, but an additional summer of director-camper estrangement remained. In 1956 the Board hired its second choice, Saul Diament, despite misgivings that his background as a European refugee might make for difficulties in communication.

Recruiting was up; 16 high school students were selected to travel to nearby Winsted, Connecticut. There, correspondence between Henry Kohn and Governor Abraham Ribicoff had resulted in a rarity – a project to be selected without AFSC influence. The project came out of newspaper headlines; extensive flooding had dislocated families throughout the town and volunteer help to help the stranded and ease the shortages seemed an ideal undertaking.

Instead, the group endured a certain amount of disorganization. Most of the work had been accomplished by federal and state relief forces and local contractors by the time AJSS arrived. The local contractors, eager to make use of the government money, pressured the city government to renege on their original commitment to allow the AJSS to engage in construction. Thus, there was no real work supervision, and instead Diament had to scramble to find work. The labor that was done – digging trenches, landscaping, cutting overgrowth, and painting a local YMCA – might have been valuable but seemed too random and scattered to make the campers feel they had accomplished meaningful change.

The housing crisis hit home. The prearranged living quarters in the local YMCA had the group coming a bit too close on a daily basis to infirm and intrusive older men; after two weeks Kohn arranged for new living quarters in an old house. Then the well gave out, and the campers had to make do with bottled water. Any project director would have been at a disadvantage. The group dug and built its own privy; only this allowed the project to continue until its scheduled departure date.

The post-summer letters of the campers accuse the project director of poor planning, weak leadership, and disinterest in the group. Even a volunteer who identified the summer as the best of her life, a claim soon to repeated yearly, thought the director was ineffective.[26]

Still, even a poor relationship with the director and weak administration of the work could not dampen the idealistic zeal some of the group channeled into their activity.

In a long feature article in the *New York World-Telegram and Sun*, camper Rachel Stern told reporter Sally McDougall, "We wouldn't know what to do on an idle summer vacation, just looking for ways to have a selfish good time. This is fun, but it's different. There's satisfaction in knowing we are helping others. We're having a wonderful time."[27]

Whatever grumblings AJSS campers expressed about administrators in their post-summer letters to Kohn, positive sentiments regarding their accomplishments were recorded as well. Despite cavils about too much authority from older members of the early groups, all the volunteers expressed pride in their work. Michael Clarke, one of those who finished his summer without a project director, was profoundly moved by his work at the Highlander Folk School. He has become a board member of the AJSS and continues to remain in personal contact with Henry Kohn from his retirement home in Florida.[28]

Of the early AJSS project directors, none had been as committed to the AFSC model of committee decisions and thorough discussion as Hy and Nora Sankel. Moreover, Hy Sankel's experience as a teacher and principal of high school youth indicated his ability and ease with working with adolescents. The Sankels availability in 1957 marked an end to directorial instability.

Indeed 1957 can be considered the year the organization came of age. Despite the initial difficulty of finding a site (reflected in ads in several New York City newspapers and a *World-Telegram* article entitled, "Teens' Work Bid Gets No Takers"[29]), the organization could be proud of the conjunction of several positive elements: a cohesive, adequately sized group (12 high school students, 10 from the New York metropolitan area), meaningful work, spirited discussion and a full commitment to open communication between directors and campers.

The selection was unusual. The organization traveled to Yellow Springs, Ohio to build a two-classroom school building for a nature center operated by Antioch College. Surrounding public school districts used the Glen Helen educational center to enrich educational opportunities for their students but neither the school districts nor Antioch had budgeted the funds to pay for the expansion. The group stayed in lodges built by the AFSC in previous summers. When the AJSS finished its contribution, the center would educate and house 80 children, and Antioch was committed to providing two teachers. The lumber was donated from a dismantled army barracks.[30]

The living situation made group cohesion easier, since the AJSS contingent lived alone in the lodges; so private and secluded did the group feel that one drowsy camper, up at dawn to accomplish some early work, hid under the couch in fear when the door was opened by the milkman.

The Sankels instituted a regular Monday evening meeting to talk out issues; they made the campers feel empowered enough to address concerns. One such meeting added a ten-minute break from work in both morning and afternoon work shifts. It worked. Antioch Director of Continuing Education wrote to Henry Kohn, thanking the group for its 2950 hours of labor. "We would not have had them [the facilities] really ready for another year, if then."

The letters to Kohn that September reflected a range of feelings, but the number of raves was unprecedented. "This past summer has been a meaningful experience in terms of my own personal development and left me with a deep feeling of responsibility to my fellow man (which I like), a sensitivity to the needs of those whom I am associated with, and a realization that the ethical concepts and beauty of Judaism are to be experienced every day of one's life," wrote Richard Lazer, who concluded that he found "joy in performing service for others."

Other comments were more concise but no less enthusiastic. Ann Dee Margulies felt, "This summer was the best I have ever had," Julian Goldsmith [he of the fear of the milkman] had his "greatest summer," and Marjorie Fetter expressed her gratitude this way: "I don't know how to thank the AJSS enough."[31]

The return of the Sankels symbolized the elements of a successful summer: meaningful work, experienced educators of adolescents as project directors who were capable of fostering a coherent group identity, and a volunteer group of at least ten with a close age range. Having weathered the early storms of its organizational spring, the AJSS now organized for summers in a changing America beginning to address inequities in economic, racial, and gender relations. The service projects would inevitably interact with the great domestic issues facing the United States.

3

Encountering Black America

The changing demographics of American society have often led the dominant majority to ignore the injunction in *Leviticus* to remember and to share with the stranger. Successive generations of immigrants from increasingly alien lands have been met more frequently with violent hostility than with welcoming generosity. The massive southern and eastern European immigration of 1880-1920 (from which most American Jews trace their lineage), was halted by the xenophobic and isolationist congress of the 1920s, seeking to protect the white Protestant majority from hordes of Catholics, Eastern Orthodox, and Jewish aliens engulfing the cities of the east. More recent immigrations from Asia and Latin America have been equally unwelcome.

But no stranger has been more savagely abused and consistently denied than those descended from the forced immigration of the slave trade. As historian Edmund S. Morgan has eloquently documented, the success of the Virginia colony, which nurtured the revolutionary democratic and republican thinking of Washington, Jefferson, Patrick Henry and Madison, was made possible only by the imprisoned labor of stolen Africans, whose living conditions and very mortality were irrelevant to the European colonists thriving on subjugation.[1] Emancipation from slavery was replaced by violent disenfranchisement in the south and marginalization, often enforced with violence, throughout the United States. Nearly one hundred years ago, W.E.B. DuBois warned the nation that "the problem of the twentieth century is the problem of the color line."[2] As the twenty-first century dawns, America's most pressing domestic concern remains erasing the vicious intolerance and inequality, the biblical inequity, which is still the heritage of slavery.

The American Jewish Society for Service initiated its activity precisely as black citizens began forcing the American majority to redress grievances. Black veterans of the war against fascism were increasingly unwilling to accept passively an imposed inferiority. Presidential desegregation of the armed forces and the voters' rejection of Dixiecrat Strom Thurmond in the 1948 election were early signs of the changes to come. The integration of baseball made bigger headlines, as well it should: In Jackie Robinson's acceptance of a two-year moratorium on answering the racist slurs thrown at him, he was providing a model of the non-violent resistance to come. Similarly, his outspoken confrontation of all foes beginning in 1949 would presage the militant nationalism of the Student Non-Violent Coordinating Committee and the Black Panther party after 1965.

More than half of the projects undertaken by the AJSS in the early years were aimed at providing help for black citizens. In hooking up with Flanner House in Indianapolis or the Morningside Community Center's camps in New Hampshire, AJSS, following the tradition of the Friends, was making an early commitment to attacking America's most grievous inequity. This was not a conscious political act; the organization went where it was invited or followed the path blazed by the AFSC. Perhaps the preponderance of projects including black Americans occurred because only cutting edge groups would work with a collection of teenage Jews from New York. Whatever the reason, AJSS contingents often witnessed or participated in the massive social change in race relations in the United States. The bond made between the tiny contingent in Indianapolis and the residents building a whole new neighborhood was perhaps the most positive outcome of the initial summer. The group undertook intentional pioneering in race relations. As project director Irwin Stark noted,

> Campers were seen in Douglas Park, reserved for Negroes, where they were probably the first white people to use the park's segregated swimming pool. They met scores of Negroes at Flanner House and hundreds of others at the Indiana State Federation of Colored Women's Clubs. In the neighborhood they were recognized on the street and answered many a friendly "Hi, neighbor!" as they returned begrimed and exhausted from a day's work.[3]

The campers became closest to the 21 black men working to build their own houses on the self-help project. Most moving was the completion of a home for a legless black veteran, who moved into his new habitat while the project was in operation. The experiences of these men with a racist society provided a better education than the group could have had from any book.

> One man told how he had broken in a white boy on his job only to watch the latter given the foreman's position which should rightfully have been given to him, an incident to which should be appended the postscript that subsequently the colored man was elected shop steward in a predominately white section of the plant. And campers witnessed another incident which highlighted the color relationship unforgettably: a white truck driver drove his vehicle down the main street of the project in defiance of a city ordinance, and a Negro project worker, a husky ex-GI, pointed to the warning sign, but the truck driver only yelled a scornful "Go to Hell!" and, while the Negro stood there choking back his fury, drove complacently to his destination.[4]

AJSS campers who extended their stay in New Hampshire to become counselors at Rabbit Hollow did it to strengthen the bonds they had formed with the youngsters they assisted.

With the 1955 project at Tennessee's Highlander Folk School, AJSS was hooking up with a nurturing cradle of the civil rights movement. As civil rights historian Taylor Branch writes, since the early 1930s,

> Highlander had functioned as a unique "workshop" of the Social Gospel, being one of the few places in the South where Negroes and whites mixed freely. Its founder, Myles Horton, had been a student of Reinhold Niebuhr at Union Theological Seminary. Niebuhr was chairman of the Highlander advisory board that at times included Eleanor Roosevelt, Norman Thomas, and Harry Emerson Fosdick.[5]

Just before the AJSS visited Highlander, Mississippi Senator James O. Eastland, seeking to invoke the hysterical anti-communism of the era to defend Jim Crow, had used his chairmanship of the Senate Internal Security Subcommittee of the Judiciary Committee to smear the school as a communist conspiracy.

From Eastland's standpoint there was indeed a conspiracy: open preparation to challenge and destroy segregation, restrictions on voting, and all aspects of southern inequality. In the early 50s, a young activist named Septima Clark came for training, and as the decade continued, workshops on non-violence were attended or led by James Lawson and Martin Luther King, Jr. A few years later, resident folk singer Guy Carawan and guest Pete Seeger worked with gospel singers to refigure old hymns into civil rights anthems. Among the songs to emerge from Highlander workshops was *We Shall Overcome*. The increased activity brought increased attack. Though struggling on for many years, Highlander would finally be forced to close after years of prosecution on trumped up bootlegging charges.[6]

At the height of the frenzied denunciation of Highlander, Henry Kohn followed AFSC and Unitarian efforts and arranged for an AJSS project to repair the property and dig trenches for new plumbing facilities. One of the activities included the building of an elaborate fence to demarcate Highlander's property and to protect it from encroachment from hostile neighbors. Kohn's own confident detachment from hysteria was made possible after he called the staunchly anti-Communist American Jewish Committee, which verified his hunch that Eastland's red-baiting was a sham.[7]

Living in tents and facing the lush, green hills of Tennessee, the group completed several projects: landscaping an athletic field, repairing and maintaining the wells, erecting fencing, and constructing a dock and raft. Mostly isolated from the activities of the school, and often without a strong education program because of the inexperience of project director Morton Kanter, the campers nonetheless found civil rights an important subtext of the summer. Members of the Chattanooga synagogue "explained" to AJSS campers that they objected to integration of the schools because "the colored people frequently had no opportunity to bathe." When Chattanooga families returned the campers' visit, they were the first neighbors to visit the school in its more than twenty year history. Thus, the AJSS project was the first bridge between the school and the surrounding community.

Septima Clark, beginning a several summer stay at Highlander during which she would offer training to John Lewis and other Nashville activists that would prove vital to the 1960 sit-down movement, took a personal interest in the small Jewish enclave at the school. At a dance where the AJSS campers stood on the outside, Clark dazzled camper Michael Clarke, insisting they must be family, despite the extra "e" on the boy's name. As they joined arms, Septima Clark guessed, "This is about the first time you've ever danced with a black lady, isn't it?" Clark was delighted when her hunch was confirmed; she had found yet another way to bridge the racial divide.

On a daily basis, individual campers attended Highlander seminars advocating social change in the rural south, participating in the same training as the civil rights leadership that transformed the nation. Among this group was Hillel Halkin, the well-known Hebrew translator and literary figure.[8]

At Highlander, Kohn and the AJSS had not been deterred by the attacks of powerful senators on the school. A few years later, AJSS aided another integrated school surrounded by hostile neighbors. This time, the local Jewish residents were among those who feared the society's presence.

By 1959 the south was increasingly polarized. Early successes in Montgomery, Alabama after the 1955-1956 bus boycott and the 1958 desegregation of Little Rock, Arkansas schools had broadened the appeal of the emerging civil rights movement and intensified the reaction of those clinging to segregation. White Citizens' Councils were the organizational embodiment of the stiffening resistance, and the older instruments of terror like the Ku Klux Klan staged television rallies to advertise their allegiance to intimidation.

Jewish organizations like B'nai B'rith's Anti-Defamation League and the American Jewish Congress proclaimed widespread support for the desegregation effort. Jews often identified with black struggles against racism because the cultural tradition of both groups celebrated liberation of slavery and because white supremacy echoed the racist motifs of Nazism. For a passionate group of AJSS volunteers, the freedom struggle of the late 1950s and early 1960s was the most important cause in the nation.

The Penn Center on St. Helena Island, Frogmore, South Carolina had been pioneering against racism for almost 100 years. Founded by abolitionists to bring literacy to former slaves, it had become a trade center for people of any color; in the racially polarized 1950s this meant most of the students were black. The school also had a conference center that hosted public events aimed at fostering integration. In 1955 the AFSC had sponsored a project there. In 1959, Elly and Ruth Saltzman initiated 35 years of AJSS experience as project directors or executive directors by bringing a group to work on the conference center. Originally, the plan for the seven-week program was to build a new dock for swimming and boating. The work proceeded so quickly that eventually additional activities were proposed and accomplished, including demolishing of a barn, transplanting trees, clearing and seeding fields, maintaining building floors and constructing fireplaces. The contentious issue that created conflict within the group was: Now that there is a dock, who should swim by it?

Penn Center's Director, Courtney Siceloff, was named to the South Carolina Advisory Committee to the US Commission on Civil Rights shortly before the group arrived. He was intensely hated by the white power structure of South Carolina, and proponents of the old order looked upon his school with contempt and fury. When Saltzman traveled to Frogmore for his spring orientation trip, he was startled to discover that the 35 family Jewish congregation in Beaufort, just seven miles west of the school, was apprehensive about the AJSS' arrival. Eventually the president of the congregation would tell the group, "There were times when we hid our Torah from month to month for fear of violence and bombings." Before the summer, temple members explained that while they recognized "that our purpose was noble and just . . .there would be many factions in the south that would reinterpret our good intentions. Fear ran high that harm would come [to them] during or after our stay at Penn Community Center." Thus, "we were not welcomed officially."[9] The anxiety in the Jewish community was reflected in contradictory telephone conversations with Henry Kohn. Before committing to the Penn Center project, Kohn spoke with the congregation; he was assured an AJSS contingent would be welcomed. By mid-June, after all arrangements had been made, some temple members grew wary; they called and asked for the project to be cancelled. Kohn explained that commitments to both Penn Center and the volunteers mandated that the project would go ahead.[10]

Now that the dock was finished, the AJSS campers wanted to swim alongside black youngsters and adults learning at the school. The fact that South Carolina law forbade integrated swimming in no way deterred the young volunteers; in fact defying Jim Crow was more of an incentive than cooling off in the water. Siceloff admired the idealism of the volunteers, but Saltzman could hardly encourage young people for whom he was responsible to engage in activity that might have them arrested. When the summer was over, he characterized his group:

> Our "kids," as they like to be called, are very ethical and idealistic minded. They come to us from varied backgrounds and a variety of states. They are conformist in practice but oppose organized religion. They are adolescents but work as hard as any adult. They will argue over the relative merits of Kashrut and balk at the prospect of a Sabbath morning service. They attended the Baptist churches on St. Helena Island with enthusiasm and anxiety. They are overly friendly toward the Negro but look down with contempt upon the Hassidim for

their antiquated dress and customs. They are with hopes for mankind
and peace but see around them an intolerable situation of race relations.[11]

Several of the campers became aroused to the point of threatening civil
disobedience not only against South Carolina, but against AJSS restrictions as well.
Henry Kohn counseled all that it was not the organization's job to change the law,
only to provide service, and he arranged that Siceloff publicly agree that
desegregation of the new dock be held off until after the group departed. Several
campers wrote steamy letters home and some of the parents wrote or called Kohn
in New York. Unflappable as ever, the AJSS President replied that having idealistic
campers upset by racial injustice was to be expected, even welcomed.

The theme of combating racial injustice was not always divisive. The whole
contingent was appalled at being prevented from observing a movie from the balcony,
which was reserved for black residents *only*. When a collection of local youth
challenged AJSS members with a version of *Dixie*, counselor Mel Moss galvanized
the group by replying with the *Battle Hymn of the Republic*. Education events
included speakers from the Southern Regional Council on Race Relations and a
local chapter of the Anti-Defamation League.

To mend fences with the local congregation, Rabbi Hoffman conducted a
service with Saltzman acting as cantor, which he continued to do throughout the
stay. He was asked to return and perform this function during Rosh Hashanah and
Yom Kippur. The synagogue members had reason for apprehension. As the 20-
hour bus trip back to New York was about to depart, Siceloff confided in Saltzman
that the local state senator had mentioned to him "that he had kept his eye on this
bunch of rabble-rousing Jewish communists since their arrival."

Every group of campers is different. A conclave of idealists who wish to
change the world, the type Elly and Ruth Saltzman brought to the Penn Center,
might be followed by a parochial and wary grouping the next. Similar dynamics –
and opposite ones – were experienced by Ed and Annette Cohen in 1962, when the
AJSS returned to Indianapolis to work again for Flanner House.

Now the self-help organization had already built 80 homes, but the
reception was no longer as welcoming. Cohen had to scramble at the last minute
when the arranged housing proved inadequate (Hardly the first or the last time
project directors have been forced to improvise). Some of the campers were upset
when the girls were propositioned by a few of the young married black men working
beside the campers to construct wall sections and tresses as part of their sweat
equity in Flanner House.[12]

> The fears that some of our campers openly expressed for
> Negroes was beaten down and destroyed in many ways. When we held
> a twist party and some Negro builders were invited, a few in the group
> openly opposed this kind of contact. Afterwards, they expressed relief
> and were glad that their fears were being replaced by images of people.

> After three weeks teenagers finally made contact with the local Negro teenagers. Healthy activities such as films, tennis and parties seemed to reinforce all these positive feelings for their fellow man. Discriminatory generalizations slowly began to disappear. Many of our campers believed, theoretically and morally, as so many of us, in integration. Yet how any of us could actually put this into practice? A summer in Indianapolis, 1962, gave us the conviction and the faith that unity of mankind was a reality to be achieved and not just mouthed.[13]

Flanner House provided an education for all the participants in the AJSS project, the Cohens included. The impressive, well-organized operation was entirely run by people of color, most of them university intellectuals. Though New Yorkers, the Cohens "had never met blacks who were so well educated."[14]

Another kind of first was achieved that summer. For his campers and for himself, Ed Cohen remembers, "I had never had blacks personalize what they went through as blacks." One such experience was related by the daughter of a Flanner House director, who described how not long before, she and a group of her teenage friends went to an A&W outlet and waited over an hour for service, while noticing that white customers who arrived much later were coming and going while they were unattended. Her group made clear its intention to stay until served, and finally, they reluctantly were offered the famous root beer. But instead of being served in the large trademark mugs, the black pioneers were served in paper cups, leaving the unmistakable impression that the soda outlet's staff was afraid their precious mugs would be "contaminated."

The group drove south of Indianapolis – what Cohen remembers as "red neck country" with Flanner House director Bill Barber. They were trailed and then pulled over by a local police officer, though they had violated no law. Barber and the AJSS group saw this as intimidation because the car was integrated, and they felt no summons was issued because Barber had many political and university connections in town which he made known to the officer.

The Cohen's five year old son was also experiencing a new world. Attending day camp as the only white child, he played happily and one night wondered when he could bridge the difference between himself and his playmates. He asked his parents, "When does white turn to black?"

Living as New Yorkers in the most heterogeneous city in the world did not mean the Jewish youngsters had three-dimensional relationships with African American people back home. Within Jewish neighborhoods, blacks were most often seen in a relationship which was both intimate and unequal, as day maids inside middle class Jewish homes. While employers might be free of conscious racism, the condescension involved in hiring another to clean and order one's private space does not create an open give-and-take between equals. By the early 1960s, this was one of the factors increasing black-Jewish tensions cited by Nathan Glazer and Daniel Patrick Moynihan in their famous study of New York ethnic groups, *Beyond the Melting Pot.* (They also referred to ethnic inequalities in the garment unions, resentment of Jewish employers by black workers, and the presence of many Jewish landlords in neighborhoods that were once Jewish and were now increasingly black and Hispanic. These factors were unlikely to be part of the consciousness of the volunteers.)[15]

The Cohens' policy of inviting local folks to dinner and encouraging social functions like dances broke down many barriers. When the summer was over, many of the campers, whose only experience with black people had been with domestics in their suburban homes, thanked the Cohens for dissipating their fears.[16]

A transformation of this type would have been enough to be proud of. Ironically, Cohen soon found himself cast, like Saltzman in 1959, as an obstacle preventing progress. When a talk given by a local NAACP official included a description of a projected civil disobedience campaign, several of the campers insisted they participate. Once again, an AJSS project director had to establish a boundary on idealism to prevent arrest. This time, though some grumbled publicly, privately many admitted they were relieved at their director's intercession.[17]

That same summer, campers on another site expressed their own troubled awareness of developing tensions between Jews and blacks. By now CBS News had "discovered" the "Black Muslims," and the young Jewish idealists, committed to an end to bigotry, expressed their fears of anti-Semitism among African Americans at an education evening in Palatine, Illinois in August 1962.

Jules and Julianne Hirsh, initiating 26 summers as project directors, led a second consecutive project to improve the facilities of Camp Reinberg which brought inner city youngsters out of Chicago to enjoy summers in the country. One night an opinionated group of AJSS campers challenged Regina H. Saxton, director of a local YWCA and a local black activist, on the subject of the political direction of "the Negro." She enjoyed the meeting of minds, but she was concerned enough about encouraging the thought of the group to write a letter the next day, summarizing her views. Reminding her readers that there is a difference between what "the Jew" thinks about [captured Nazi Adolph] Eichmann (then on trial in Jerusalem for genocide) and what "you" as an individual think about Eichmann, Saxton continued:

> Remember that Negroes are *people*. They feel, think, act – in many ways. We aren't going to change our behavior toward each other unless we can see *persons* on the Freedom March; persons in the Muslim [sic] movement, persons who live 'in the persons of their skin' – and who do all the wonderful, reprehensible, thoughtless and tender things that members of the human race do. Now you must use every opportunity to get at the personal. That's a pretty big task I'm giving you – but one I think you can do. It will not be easy. You will sometimes be rebuffed, looked at with suspicion and resented.
>
> But if you really are sincere in trying to know the person, *you* are going to be involved in the *encounter*. You are going to look at

yourself. It is in these moments in our relatedness to each other that we grow.[19]

The truth of Ms. Saxton's letter is demonstrated by scores of personal relationships AJSS campers have developed over the years with sponsors, work supervisors, home owners, and support personnel. These contacts have time and again broached the gulf between themselves and "the stranger." The testimony of 1993 Selma, Alabama cook Ruby Fuller about the Selma voter registration drive was far more profound because the campers already loved her cooking and knew her as person of rare humanity. Despite her own borderline economic status, Fuller has for years cared for young people of every color who have been mistreated or abandoned by their families. Doing demolition for an old house to make way for a Habitat home, Selma volunteers were awed by the dedication and power of William Millhouse, brother of the homeowner. His decency, dynamism, and ready friendship made the notion of sweat equity powerful.[20]

As the militancy of the civil rights movement was transformed by black nationalism, white participants—many of whom were Jewish—found themselves increasingly unwelcome. This had negligible impact on AJSS summers because the society did not work for self-conscious civil rights organizations (The visit to Highlander was a notable exception), but instead aided church-based service organizations and as the sixties progressed, local groups funded by federal anti-poverty dollars. Most of these projects were in small, rural communities, where black and white residents were getting their first look at Jews. Those being helped by the work were discovering that for the young people they encountered, Judaism meant aiding one's neighbor. The polarization AJSS contingents encountered was more likely to be between the organization it was aiding and a hostile white community. By the late 1960s, AJSS campers often found that those maintaining racial inequity were also Vietnam war hawks, while most of the campers identified with the campus anti-war movement they were only a year from joining.

Sometimes the contrast between the welcome of a local black community and the hostility of the white population was the single sharpest memory retained from the summer. During the contentious summer of 1968, Jules and Julianne Hirsh led a group to isolated Clinton, Kentucky. The host organization, the Community Action Program, was only 16 months old and was the brainchild of an out-of-state anti-poverty organizer named Michael Shapiro. The Hirshes flatly reported, "The majority of the white community despised him," and absolutely no cooperation from local officials was advanced. A rural community, the town had a central square where the only black people seen were waiters in the café. Idle white men sat in the town square shooting at black birds roosting on the roofs and expressing strong support for George Wallace's presidential campaign. Most of the black population lived on farmhouses, but there was a minority section of town, set literally on the other side of the railroad tracks from the village center. The schools had been integrated for only three years and were still smoldering with resentment.

Counselor Rhonda Kirschner remembers being welcomed by two separate receptions. At the first, attended by several of the hamlet's more affluent white members, Kirschner was approached by a proud middle class woman who related that when she told her neighbor she was going to a reception for "those Jewish people," her neighbor was puzzled. "Do they speak English?" she wanted to know.

At the reception by the black community, there was great warmth but also sobering information, as 5 to 7 year old children talked without visible emotion of the deaths of their one month or one year old siblings, with enough frequency that academic discussions of differing child mortality rates was replaced by grim personal reality.[21]

The task of the summer was repairing and painting houses in 81 homes and churches in four counties. This included painting, repairing roofs, erecting new walls and ceilings, repairing and rebuilding porches, and enlarging two homes. The homes were memorable: at several Kirschner was startled to look through the walls to see patches of blue sky – in places where there were no windows. A schedule that kept the volunteers in a particular town for one of two days mandated quick work. Nonetheless, "The bond of kinship that was established was so strong that this was a most important plus for all of our experiences... The white community was very suspicious of our presence. The rumors were varied and while it was never said to us, we felt their thoughts, 'The Jews are helping the Negroes.'"

> Our relationship with the black community on the other hand was one of true brotherhood. Our campers were so well received that the presence of racial differences was non-existent. When we visited the community center (the building was the Negro school before integration) the community prepared a chicken dinner for our group. Our boys and girls spent many hours at the community center, dancing, playing ball and just talking. I feel that it was the contact with our campers that prompted some of the young Negro leaders to try to gain admission to the Clinton swimming pool. While walking in the white section of town I sometimes felt uncomfortable about peoples' reaction to our group, but I never felt that in the black section of town . . . This was perhaps the strongest rapport between an AJSS group and a community group. I attribute the tremendous overall success of the summer to this close bond of brotherhood.[22]

Success of a more limited and personal kind occurred with at least one white person. While white teenagers the group encountered at a church dance promised to show up at the worksite, they never did, but a strange and ultimately satisfying encounter between Jules and a local entrepreneur proved incremental progress could be made even with "a good old boy."

When the Hirshes drove into Clinton, arriving as project directors always do a day or two before the group to set up shop, Jules pulled into the gas station and told the proprietor in a rebel hat that he was looking for the Community Action

Center. Where was it or Mike Shapiro? He was met by silence, though the owner exchanged money and change for gasoline. After successfully hunting down Shapiro on their own, the Hirshes were settled into housing two and a half blocks from the gas station. "We were housed in an old vacant home which was literally falling apart. Plaster was falling off the ceilings, paper from the wall, floors were termite ridden, plumbing deplorable. Showers had to be taken in bathing suits, outside, with a garden hose since there was only one bathtub, no shower for the entire group."[23] Jules put down planking so his daughter Alexandria's crib wouldn't fall through the floorboards. He rigged up a Rube Goldberg contraption with the hose outside to try to get hot showers. Only five people would exhaust the water supply, so they drew lots. All through the summer, the Hirshes continued to buy gas from the silent owner and even arranged to have his car serviced there. A stuffed toilet led to a new catastrophe: the plumbing line was broken and the repair would take days. Jules walked over to gas station and addressed his taciturn acquaintance. "I know we don't speak, but I'm going to find out just what kind of a man you are." Jules reminded the man that his boys and girls were doing Good Work. He explained about the toilets and then demanded the keys to the boys and girls rest rooms. After looking at Hirsh for a few seconds, the gas station owner retreated to his office and returned holding both keys, silently handing them over. "Thank you," said Jules.

Breaking his wall of silence, the service station owner looked the AJSS project director squarely in the eye. "It's OK," he said.[24]

The following summer, Carl and Audrey Brenner led a group into impoverished Ripley, Tennessee. As at the William Penn Center, the labor included restoring a swimming facility, this time a pool in a community center at the behest of the project sponsor, the Ripley Economic Support Association. But ten years was a long time in the south – at least legally. When the work was completed, the AJSS contingent dove in – the first white people ever to swim in the formerly black pool. By 1969 of course, all local segregation laws were legally dead, though the campers had seen a colored waiting room when they arrived at the bus station.

However, one must agree with the Brenners' current assessment that "We didn't know what dangers we were in." While the living conditions for the group were primitive – only the girls and the Brenners slept inside a small building, while the boys tented on the lawn – their work aroused the anger of the local redneck population. Apparently this element resented the work, which mainly consisted of home repair on shacks so primitive they had dirt floors and no indoor plumbing or electricity. Some of the structures had previously been hay silos. Most of the labor was building porches as refuges from the summer heat. Or perhaps it was the outspoken opposition to the war in Vietnam that campers expressed at a public meeting. Even the black residents were fearful of anti-war views, quickly exiting the meeting when the war became the hot topic. In any case, revenge was taken after the AJSS contingent left town: the building the group stayed in was burned down.[25]

Through the seventies, tensions between black and white neighbors in the rural south continued. Sometimes the presence of the AJSS was a key factor in bridging gaps within a divided community. A wealthy black contractor who had ignored the activity of the South East Mississippi Community Action Center in Hattiesburg and was a high school classmate of the SEMCA director only contributed lumber and other materials to the organization after he hosted the 1978 AJSS contingent to a dinner and was impressed by the purposefulness of the group.[26]

Not that people were always receptive. That same summer, work supervisor Alvin Dahmer, whose father had been murdered by racists in retribution for his civil rights activism, consistently underestimated the ability and dedication of the campers. He "often seemed antagonistic to what we were doing. He did not understand our continued emphasis on having enough work and supervision for the group at all times... On the last day of work when there was nothing to do, Mr. Dahmer expressed a sincere appreciation for the service rendered by the group. He felt it was amazing that we had done as much as we had and expressed his regret that the community had not done more for the group."[27]

In areas outside the south, black neighborhoods were not always welcoming. In Waterloo, Iowa, the Hirshes reported that despite their broad hints, no invitations to attend individual or organizational functions were forthcoming.[28]

In the rural south, the astounding contrast between impoverishment and plenty included ignorance of how modern facilities worked. A 1974 project in Opelika, Alabama provided an opportunity for mutual education in the realities of life. The journey to the work site was a daily battle with a mud road and potholes. For several days a dead horse lay in the road. The owner had no means to remove it, possessing only two other horses and a plow. He had to wait until a neighbor with a tractor could take a break from his work to pull the equine away. The Alabama Council on Human Relations provided housing at a Head Start center where the campers slept on mattresses on the floor surrounded by the red clay dust from outside. Plumbing facilities were provided to many families for the first time, but the group had to educate one family about the use of a toilet. Unlike Ruthie and Winfield Joad in *The Grapes of Wrath*, who feared they'd broken the amenity in a government camp when they heard it flush,[29] these folks had been afraid to pull the handle. They had been removing and dumping the feces in a hog field outside.[30]

If black-Jewish relations were under strain nationwide, AJSS campers found the most memorable counterpoint in the scores of human relationships they developed among those who lived in the homes being built or renovated.

Testimony about what the value of human contact means in being responsive to "the stranger" was eloquently summarized by campers Michael Kaplan and Rachel Frankel, writing of their 1978 Mississippi summer:

> After six weeks of volunteer work in the poverty stricken black neighborhoods of Hattiesburg, we found that there was another side of Judaism than what religious school taught us. We have come to realize

that attending Shabbat services regularly, knowing all the prayers, keeping kosher, making large cash contributions to the synagogue, and putting a mezuzah on your door are not the only signs of a Jew. After working with and for the less fortunate citizens of Hattiesburg, we learned how rewarding physical contributions, a giving of ourselves, can be. This is called "tzedakah." We found this aspect of Judaism is widely overlooked by Jews and gentiles alike. We feel that by coming to Hattiesburg we have fulfilled one of the most important tenets of Judaism. We feel that not only have we learned more about the goodness inside our soul but we feel that the community has also benefited from it.

To us Judaism means: Giving Mrs. Moselle Tate a new paint job for her kitchen and bedroom, making benches and picnic tables for Toby and Junior, helping Mrs. Paige feel more secure in her home by installing doors with locks, giving Boris a water fountain, roofing Mrs. Williamson's house so that she will be able to stay dry when it rains, providing shelters for Mabelle and Sonya when the sun is high in the sky, and of course, extending ourselves to the kids at Currie Street Park and making new friends.[31]

Campers could be humbled by the decency and faith of some of those they aided. In Alice, Texas, AJSS volunteers weatherized homes for the elderly. Though they had been working on such projects for 18 years, the Hirshes reported, "The condition of the homes was among the worst we have ever seen. One, owned by an elderly black lady, Suzie Miller, had been without water, gas and electricity for several months. Mrs. Miller's plight deeply affected the members of our group. We installed a water system, replaced all the windows, built a new front porch, and cleaned up her property."[32]

Ruth Sod, a camper in Alice, discussed the impact of Mrs. Miller on her group:

Even though I was learning new skills, I could still not comprehend the good deeds I was doing for these people. What I think opened my eyes was when we arrived at 1223 S. Wright Street. As Sam's pickup came to a stop at the front of this broken down house, I remember the sinking feeling that came over me. We had been working on homes that were in livable condition but this was by far the worst. There were piles of junk and garbage outside which exemplified the condition of the house. The screens were all torn and the windows, if intact, were immovable. As I approached the entrance, an unpleasant odor hit me. I later learned there was no flushing toilet. I saw a woman with a look of dignity and wisdom, sitting in an aged rocker which set the scene for the room. The room was run down and had a very depressed feeling about it. The woman's name was Suzie Miller. She lived with her granddaughter Barbara and two of her great grandchildren, Wilbur and Michael. They had been living without water, electricity, and gas for about five months. There were many holes in the walls from a recent fire in the house, which her husband had built. The entire house was infested with bugs and small rodents. Still Mrs. Miller survived at the age of 88.

We all became Mrs. Miller's friends. We heard stories of her childhood. Throughout all of our conversations with her she never conveyed to us that she was unhappy. She realized that she would never have enough money to fix her home and she praised the Lord that we had come. It was at this moment that I realized why I was here. I saw this poor woman, with no money and terrible living conditions. And here I was – young, willing and able to help her and make her life better, Seeing Mrs. Miller made me realize why I had come.[33]

Magnetic personalities of venerable black women dominated several projects. Mrs. Latham, feisty and faithful in her mid-80s, made the 1975 Greenville, North Carolina group pray with her each morning before renovation of her house would begin. She was appreciative: "You Jews know how to show your religion by the work that you do to help us folk." She was also determined that the young volunteers should succeed. "Don't act like a nigger," she warned them. "Get your education." Mrs. Latham came to New York for the fall reunion, and the Hirshes took her to the United Nations.[34]

Of course, there was no guarantee attitudes would change. The Hirshes led a group to tiny Lewiston, North Carolina (population, 500) in 1982. Though officially welcomed by people of both races, the volunteers found that whites tended to keep their distance. For the farewell party, the directors invited both the white store owners and the black residents; the whites didn't come. But the grimmest education was unintentionally provided by the local tobacco baron, who arranged a tour of his farm and consistently referred to George Lee, the work supervisor in his 70s revered by the AJSS group, as "that boy." His teenage grandson told the campers how much he hated "nigger music."

The contrast between such bigotry and the friendship of the local black population created strong feelings. The Hirshes again reported that "The group felt as though they were part of the black community." Part of that feeling came through the sense of smell. The old Jim Crow school in the heart of the black neighborhood that the volunteers were converting to a community center was down wind from a Perdue chicken processing plant. Campers had to decide which stunk more: the nauseating fumes from the plant or the reported sexual harassment of the black women who worked there. The AJSS contingent was made welcome at services of the Mt. Olive Baptist Church, whose spirited congregation sent two or three members to assist the volunteers each day.[35]

Though AJSS campers were often invited to church services, the experiences over the years among southern black congregations have been most memorable. The Kopelowitz's first project was a 1972 return to Abbeville, Louisiana, where the Hirshes had led a group the summer before. Rochelle remembers the Baptist church members dressed in white, all vigorously employing identical fans distributed at the door. This was despite the miserable poverty of the Rabbit Hill neighborhood where the group was renovating homes. Each person addressed another as Mr. or Mrs. So-and-So; Rochelle speculates the formality was a dignified response to always being called by first names – or by "boy" or "girl," regardless of the age of the individual addressed by patronizing whites. Reverend Joyner spoke in rhyming chants, evoking a vigorous call and response session from the congregation. Without warning, Joyner suddenly called on "Rabbi Marty" to speak.

Thinking on his feet, the instantly ordained Jewish minister opened the bible to *Exodus* and linked the struggles of Jews and blacks to attain emancipation to a chorus of "Yes!" and "Amen, brother."[36]

Jules Hirsh, with more preparation, delivered a sermon about the AJSS in a Baptist church in Greenville, North Carolina in 1975. There too, "the music and fervor of the congregation were a new experience."[37]

The Brenners brought their group from Ripley to a Baptist revival meeting on the Mississippi River. A guest minister had been brought from Memphis, and he quickly involved the congregation in a spirited session, this time engaging individuals in direct questioning. One by one, he selected congregants and demanded, "Who woke you up?" to which he received a fervent response: "Jesus did!" Suddenly the minister turned to one of the AJSS group and again demanded, "Who woke you up?" Astonished, the volunteer pointed to Audrey Brenner and answered literally, "She did!"

The trip to the Mississippi included another kind of education. The Brenners lay their daughter Denise on a blanket; she returned to Ripley full of chiggers and had to be wiped down in Clorox to remove the insects.[38]

By the 1980s AJSS campers of high school age might look upon the civil rights movement as ancient history. But project directors in the south maintained the immediacy of the struggle by consistently inviting civil rights activists, leaders, and veterans to address the group as vital elements of the summer's education component. The 1984 Mondale-Ferraro ticket opened its presidential campaign at a Mississippi rally attended by the Hattiesburg, Mississippi contingent with addresses by the candidates and Jesse Jackson.[39] For Jules and Julianne Hirsh, "The highlight of the [1984 Dahlonega, Georgia] summer was our VIP tour of the Martin Luther King, Jr. Center for Non-Violent Social Action in Atlanta," which included a private session of 1-½ hours with Coretta Scott King, talking of the early days of the civil rights movement.[40]

The author and his wife, Catherine Kaczmarek Milkman, began their AJSS summers in Selma, Alabama, the city where violent opposition to black voter registration galvanized the nation to create and enforce the Voting Rights Act of 1965. Twenty-eight years later, two participants, Lily Thomas and Ruby Fuller, who served as the project's cook, awed the group with poignant accounts of how the early events had transformed their lives. The Selma campers retraced the steps of the marchers over the Edmund Pettus Bridge and visited churches once addressed by Reverend King. The whole summer was organized around civil rights education, with trips to the Civil Rights Memorial and the Dexter Street Church in Montgomery (home of the evening meetings during the bus boycott) and the King Center in Atlanta. But most breathtaking of all was the Civil Rights Institute in Birmingham, an interactive multi-media display of "the Pittsburgh of the south" from its origin as model Jim Crow metropolis to the site of the 1963 demonstrations that killed segregation. We moved, as all visitors do, through facsimiles of the old segregated city and walked through separate and unequal school rooms and lunch counters. We listened to a cacophony of conflicting voices opine about race relations, viewed the jail cell King occupied in May 1963 while watching police violence on TV sets in an appliance store window, and "marched" on Washington to hear the "I have a dream" speech. Across the street is the 16th Street Baptist Church, headquarters for the May 1963 demonstrations that toppled Jim Crow and site of the September 1963 Sunday morning bombing which killed four young girls.

Tensions between blacks and whites which might include the campers themselves were more likely to surface in the north. The Kopelowitzes' experience in devastated Detroit included reminders of both positive interaction and extreme polarization. Neighborhood East Area Residents undertook to save one of the few truly integrated areas left in the city. AJSS campers fully renovated two homes, including one that had been a crack house.

> Perhaps the most significant aspect of this project was our relationship with the community residents, particularly those that lived on Three Mile Drive. These were caring, loving people who were constantly concerned about us, not only as volunteers but as friends. There was a constant stream of grateful gestures, from simple "thank yous" to a block party at which we were the guests of honor. If there is any hope for Detroit, it lies in replicating the spirit that NEAR has engendered on this block and in the community. Recognition for NEAR and AJSS was heralded in a huge front page story in *The Detroit News*.[41]

On the other hand, though the housing was luxurious (the group stayed on 20 landscaped acres in a beautifully appointed former school for the deaf administered by the Lutheran Special Education Ministries), it was surrounded by security fencing topped with barbed wire. Getting in and out required a remote control device. Campers wanted to explore the surrounding area, an inner city slum, but it was clearly off limits, as the Kopelowitzes had been repeatedly warned before moving the group in. "Every other store" seemed to sell liquor. Decaying housing surrounded by bricks and rubble was everywhere. A new mall lay abandoned downtown because white shoppers would not make use of it. On July 4 weekend, the group walked through downtown on their way to the piers to observe a fireworks display. The inquisitive glances from passersby, many of them drunk, were hostile. Though there were no incidents, the walk was not repeated during the summer.[42]

A less dramatic sign of how poverty affects behavior was visible in Jackson, Mississippi. There the food bank AJSS campers rebuilt was much more frequently patronized at the end of the month, when the food stamps ran out.

That summer's experience provided another lesson to our campers of how Jews, too, are often seen as "the other": Klan bullet holes in the synagogue were deliberately not repaired as a reminder of the danger posed by racial and religious bigotry.[43]

Though Black-Jewish relations continue to provide conflict nationally, the issue has not been a great factor for AJSS projects, where Jewish teenagers and African Americans of all ages have met on the work site and in social centers like the black church. The development of individual friendships has been the most common means of breaching the racial divide.

Perhaps the greatest impact of AJSS labor with an organization aimed at aiding the black poor was felt in four summers working with the Southern Mutual Help Association, under the leadership of the late Sister Anne Catherine Bizalion, whom the Hirshes described as "a dynamo of energy and a super champion of social justice."[44] Originally a director for Headstart in the earliest days of the War on Poverty,[45] she was so impatient with the bureaucratic pace of change that she was fired. She created SMHA and dedicated her efforts to cleaning up the horrific living conditions of the black residents of unincorporated Rabbit Hill, which the white citizenry of Abbeville, Louisiana deliberately excluded from the town so as to be not responsible for city services.

Rabbit Hill reeked of this indifference. The city refused to provide a sewer system, so as the SMHA begin installing toilets and running water in homes, brown, rancid water ran in open trenches in front of the houses. The city refused to pave the streets, so dirt roads, unmaintained by any local authority, were the only conveyance: a heavy rain could prevent transportation for hours or days. The powerful bureaucracy of the town, which included not only the local government but also the Catholic hierarchy and the wealthy whites, was utterly indifferent. Many local potentates smiled benevolently – and ignored the problem. Two years later Julianne Hirsh recalled the scene:

> I remember the humidity of Abbeville, Louisiana, but more than that I remember the Spanish moss dripping from the trees and the Cajun French accents and the spicy Creole food and a Dominican nun whom the black people called an angel, helping them in every way after she was fired as a VISTA worker community organizer. But what I remember most about Louisiana was the day we arrived. The black community held a special prayer service to bless our project. The temperature was at least 100 degrees and the humidity almost that high. And we sat for an hour or more listening to prayers and the "Amen, yes

Lords " of the people. Then we were whisked away to the home of one of the wealthiest men in town where his family and friends relaxed around the swimming pool and I was so dumbfounded by the contrast between the prayers of the poor black people we had come to help and the insensitivity of these people who could have helped, that I spoke to no one for the rest of the afternoon.[46]

The project was to renovate some of the miserable shacks people in Rabbit Hill inhabited. In one case, the home of Lela Wilson, a heavy woman of 75, there was nothing to reclaim, so the major portion of the 1971 summer was devoted to moving her in with a relative, demolishing the existing structure, and replacing it with a four room house. The plight of Mrs. Wilson moved others in the community. Police Lieutenant Al Lopez volunteered as special work supervisor on her home and raised $500 from a local doctor to purchase the materials (the grant had been for renovation only). When the new structure was almost built, AJSS campers gave the home owner a tour of her property, pointing out the living room, kitchen and bedroom. When she saw the last room, a fully equipped bathroom, the substantial Mrs. Wilson fell to her knees, and raising her head and eyes upward, declaimed, "Lord Jesus, I'm 75 years old and now I have a toilet in my house."[47]

The volunteers formed a special bond with the work supervisor on their renovation projects, Reverend Murphy Wright. Though he had been hospitalized twice for major surgery including an operation in the spring, he continued to work away at the projects. Camper Beth David was inspired to poetic expression in the project newsletter, which was called *Murph's Here!*

Murph
        good old Murph
He was always there
        to hammer a nail
        to saw a board
        to comfort the frustrated
He sacrificed so much for us
        so we could work
        so we could be happy
        so we could feel self-satisfaction
He alone kept out spirit alive
        when the work got hard
        when the sun got hot
        when too many people didn't give a damn
He was the life of our summer
        the life of our work
        the life of our joy
        the life of our lives[48]

Sister Anne Catherine did not have patience for timidity in the face of social injustice. Determined to force Abbeville to incorporate Rabbit Hill and to provide it with the necessary social services, she arranged with Henry Kohn that AJSS would spend two successive summers improving the homes. The hope was that enough work and publicity would attend the project so that the town would have to provide up to standard sewer lines and paved roads. She was fortunate to have the Hirshes around, for Jules set out to smooth over personal difficulties in order to get the cooperation of local authorities.

The Catholic Church was the most influential non-governmental institution, but though she was a nun, Sister Anne Catherine did not get along well with Monsignor Martin, "the most influential man in Abbeville," because she could not abide his unwillingness to confront racism in his parish and perhaps because he found her a woman of too powerful a personality. She had no official relationship to Martin because as a Dominican nun her superior was located in Grenoble, France. Henry Kohn characterized her position on the political spectrum as isolating her from the mainstream: "She was so far to the left she wanted to organize everyone who was walking."[49] Once the Hirshes "motivated Father Crumley of Holy Cross Church in Lafayette" to send teenagers to work with the AJSS group, Jules got the energetic nun's permission to speak with Martin. After Hirsh expressed his feeling that both AJSS and SMHA were doing God's work in helping humanity, the project director procured the priest's consent to use Catholic auspices in getting the SMHA building materials. Hirsh spoke to Kiwanis and Rotary clubs about the nature of the work and developed a relationship with Robert Weill, a Jewish lumber company owner. After talking with Hirsh, Weill offered materials for the renovation cost free. With justice, the Hirshes concluded that "The most significant contribution of AJSS this summer was bringing together many different groups and people to assist with the Rabbit Hill project."[50]

The Kopelowitzes led their first AJSS project in Abbeville the following summer. The extreme poverty was a powerful lesson, and again the memorable stench of the open trenches, particularly on rainy days, remains with them today. The volunteers renovated and expanded a one-bedroom shack for a family of eight, adding two bedrooms and indoor plumbing. So poor was the SMHA that the AJSS demolished a garage first, and saved both lumber and nails – which the campers straightened in order to use them as materials for the expansion.

For travel in Abbeville, a white man, insisting on secrecy, sold his pickup truck to Marty for $1, on the proviso that Kopelowitz would sell it back to him for $1 when the summer was over. But he did not want it known that he was helping the Jews helping the blacks. How much he wanted it back after AJSS use is unclear: the group painted the truck psychedelic colors. Their driver for the summer was Clarence Guidry, who lived in a one room trailer with tile on the floor which Rochelle maintains was cleaner than any floor in her own house. Guidry, who was returning from a similar stint with AJSS the previous summer, developed strong ties to many in the group, which insisted on bringing the Guidry family with them on their trip to New Orleans.

Sister Anne wangled a weekly radio show on which the AJSS campers spoke of their work and the philosophy that guided it.[51] This enabled the campers to have fun while garnering more publicity.

Her hopes were fulfilled. After two AJSS summers, the city agreed to pave the roads and modernize the sewers, the Rabbit Hill community was energized, and, convinced she'd created the necessary organization and progress to sustain the community, Sister Anne Catherine took the SMHA to Jeannerette, Louisiana.[52]

Sister Anne again tried to draw rural folk into the modern age. The two employers in the small community of 5000 were Fruit of the Loom, which employed 800, and the surrounding sugar plantations. AJSS campers, joining SMHA in 1980, were involved in parallel projects. The physical work was renovating and weatherizing (against hurricanes) the shacks of plantation workers. But there was an additional responsibility as well. Each day two campers accompanied VISTA and SMHA volunteers to plantation residences to have residents fill out census information. Part of the process was explaining the importance of the count: A true census would show a population in need of funding for anti-poverty programs. In addition, now that the voting rights act had been passed, counting also meant encouraging the voter registration which might eliminate hundreds of years of powerlessness.

The plantation residences were small clusters of shacks located in the middle of the sugar fields. Volunteers would drive dozens of miles through acres of crops on barely maintained dirt roads and without warning arrive in a hamlet. For counselor Sharon Kleinbaum, this was travel through time as well as space. Without a few badly maintained cars and already antiquated "modern" farm equipment, the condition of the shacks and the people who lived in them amid staggering heat and swarming flies suggested slavery.

The car would first draw a bevy of children curious about what brought a car out their way. Kleinbaum and her campers noticed that the children included a disturbingly large number of the disabled: Down's syndrome children or kids with missing hands or the wrong number of fingers or toes. SMHA officials speculated that the high percentage of the handicaps was related to the planters' practice of flying low pesticide bearing planes through the fields with the pilots making no effort to change their elevation or the discharge of poison when they came to human habitats.

The shacks themselves shocked the volunteers, though they were a disturbingly old story for the Hirshes: frequently without electricity or floors, they offered only the most basic shelter, yet their tenants tried to dress them up with a picture or two.

The tenants, who often seemed to be wearing the only clothes they owned (the kids never wore shoes), were completely in the hands of the plantation owners, who charged rents for these miserable dwellings higher than the meager wages could afford. They were paid in scrip redeemable only in the company store which kept tally of their debt and kept most in a cycle of dependency that would not be broken.

Local white people resented the census work, undoubtedly seeing it as another conspiracy to empower those on the bottom of the social order. Once a pick-up truck sporting a rifle rack followed the census takers for several miles; the driver vented his rage with shouts attacking "communists" and "northern agitators."

Conversely the black population was gracious and brimming over with gratitude. Consistently, the AJSS contingent was invited to church services where they were recognized in the sermons and fed generously at barbecues and picnics.

In addition to being powerfully exposed to images of poverty enforced by racism, AJSS volunteers also learned a lesson in humility. Their work supervisor was a modest man of the most basic education. Yet, in the words of Kleinbaum, he was a "master teacher, an artist and a master craftsman." His own work was of the finest quality, and his ability to demonstrate skills and guide the volunteers struck each member of the group. Exposure to him and to SMHA dedication helped turn around two Long Island volunteers, who had arrived with jewelry, high heels and nail polish. At first determined not to get dirty, the two campers emerged as dedicated workers whose values had been transformed by the importance of the work, the welcome of the populace and the practical idealism of SMHA.[53]

The last joint project of AJSS and SMHA occurred in 1992 when Jonathan Hirsh and Karin Kayser brought campers to Four Corners, Louisiana to build a community center. As always, Sister Anne Catherine was thinking on many lines. Naturally, she wanted to continue the process of renovating homes to bring them to decent standards of shelter and modernization. But she also saw the center as a symbol of a *community* – not merely a series of isolated people, but a living neighborhood of mutual concern. She saw in 1992 what Flanner House had seen in 1951: bringing in a group of idealistic youngsters committed to working for people who had never received recognition from others would help generate the self-respect to create that community. As she told the AJSS fall reunion:

> The Community Center was only a dream before you came, not very believable to some people who have repeated experience of failure. Building it meant the vision was becoming reality: 4 Corners could prepare for a better future. It was a sign that other people cared for this small forgotten community. It gave confidence to 4 Corners' residents that what they are doing in planning a better future is important enough for you to come and sweat while you could have a "good time" somewhere else. It encouraged young people – young men – to get involved. They told us that it is the first time somebody really cares and believes in them. It was an occasion for 4 Corners to discover another world, yours, and to break their isolation. It helped to bring together "the other community" – farmers, State Senator, bank, churches – and

to step toward the dream of a new society in Louisiana where everyone sits around the table and speaks, regardless of race, gender, age, [and] gender affiliation.[54]

The center was built in the middle of a sugar plantation, and it was meant to be the nucleus of a new community. Shortly after the summer ended, Hurricane Andrew struck, bringing winds of over 140 miles per hour and leveling the center just weeks after its creation. But the project had been larger than the building. Having seen the center rise once, community residents believed it might rise again, and pitching in with their little available free time, community residents rebuilt their center. It was the SMHA contention that the will to replace it would not have occurred without the AJSS efforts that preceded the hurricane. One of the work supervisors, again a hearty black woman named Irma Lewis, sent a message with the crusading nun to the November meeting. "Tell them we never witnessed such a fine group of young people. Tell them we love them... They made a big difference by being here."[55]

As with Sister Anne Catherine, who died in 1997 at the age of 73, AJSS work projects have many purposes. In a fragmented and often divisive society, hundreds of young people have lent their labor to create better housing, schools, camps and community centers while banging away at racism with every grasp of a hammer.

4

All the Lost Tribes

One tragic theme of American history has been the bitter, ferocious determination to evict and eliminate, even exterminate, the first people of the Western Hemisphere by European settlers and their descendants. The English settlers of Virginia, saved from starvation by local tribes, viewed the "Indians"[1] suspiciously. As the US Commission on Human Rights puts it, the British "did not view the native population as necessary to colonial life,"[2] while the Spanish eagerly transformed Indians into serfs. European colonizers, in diction and attitude borrowed from crusaders, claimed rights to the land on the basis of "discovery," which exempted those outside "Christian civilization," i.e. the people being evicted, from ownership rights to the land they clearly occupied.

The rhetoric of the revolution seemed to augur new hope. President Washington was committed to protecting Indians from land speculators. The Northwest Ordinance, progressive in more than its original anti-slavery message, declared:

> The utmost good faith shall always be observed toward the Indians; their lands and property shall never be taken from them without their consent; and in their property, rights, and liberty, they shall never be invaded or disturbed, unless in just and lawful laws authorized by Congress; but laws founded in justice and humanity shall from time to time be made for preventing wrongs being done to them; and for preserving peace and friendship with them.[3]

Thomas Jefferson, the great American contradiction, is no less puzzling on this issue. The author of the above words was the first to suggest, after purchasing the Louisiana Territory, that land in the eastern half of the country should be transferred to white Americans and exchanged for land west of the Mississippi. His suggested Indian policy was to Christianize and assimilate the "savages." Four years after Jefferson's death Andrew Jackson pushed the Indian Removal Act of 1830 through Congress, setting the stage for the horrific Trail of Tears, thus removing the majority of the Cherokee nation, the tribe most successful and amenable to assimilation, from their thriving Kentucky, North Carolina and Tennessee homelands.[4]

Though not often knowing details, Americans now have a sense that a vast injustice was done to indigenous people as the nation expanded westward. But details are necessary to understand the depth of despair that has remained. Many of the tribes were forced to move several times, even if the topography of the new land was so different from that which was left behind that an entirely new way of life had to be invented. Punitive military force was frequently used to enforce blatant violations of past treaty provisions. In the notorious case of Wounded Knee in 1890 soldiers on horseback shot down 200 men, women, and children in the act of fleeing and were then rewarded for their efforts with twenty Congressional Medals of Honor.[5] In California, one historian writes, "Between 1850 and 1859, the federal government reimbursed the state of California $924,259 for what was basically freelance murder," as vigilantes swept down on Indian villages across rivers from settlements, killing all regardless of age or gender. Whole tribes were virtually eliminated this way. At times women were spared death so that they might live as sex slaves or prostitutes. The California Indian population before the gold rush was 150,000; after 1870, it was below 30,000. As Fergus Bordewich summarizes, "There is no dispute tribes suffered staggering losses, often as much as 90% of their total, when they came into contact with white settlers."[6]

Where deliberate killing didn't wreak havoc, the introduction of European disease to those without immunity to them was almost as destructive. Measles, whooping cough, influenza and especially smallpox had devastating impacts on tribal populations throughout the late eighteenth and early nineteenth century. The worst epidemic occurred in the plains states during the 1830s which killed about 50,000 members of 15 tribes.[7]

By the late nineteenth century the reservation system was firmly in place. There land deemed more remote and less desirable for farming was assigned to tribes in farcical treaty negotiations. The US Commission on Human Rights has concluded, "It is clear that in the taking of Indian lands any device that was deemed effective was used, including theft, fraud, deceit, and military force."[8] Military negotiators often held tribal chiefs hostage until they signed the appropriate document; if the land became more desirable later, a policy of starvation – withholding food rations was one tactic – would suffice to change the provisions. Since the Indians were not Christian, they were savages; it was permissible to brutalize brutes.

President Grant brought missionaries to civilize the heathens; many Christian sects were given free hand to establish order. Grant's regulations stipulated that "Any Indian who shall engage in the sun dance, scalp dance or war dance or in any other similar feast, so called, shall be deemed guilty of an offense" and he shall be punished by withholding rations. "Medicine men" who encouraged these rites would be jailed for 30 days.[9] This prohibition would last until 1934.

Convinced that tribal culture must be destroyed if civilization could occur, President Benjamin Harrison's administration initiated a fifty year policy of forcibly tearing children from their families and shipping them as far as hundreds of miles to attend boarding schools. There they were forbidden to practice traditional beliefs, speak in their native languages, or choose tribal clothing, jewelry, or hairstyles. English was the only permitted language; for many if the violence of the separation did not mandate scholastic failure, the alien syntax would.[10]

Virtual dictatorial control of the reservations fell into the hands of the Department of Interior's Bureau of Indian Affairs. Given the prevailing attitude that the Indian population was somehow less than human, it is not surprising that the BIA was often administered by bureaucrats who were bored, incompetent, or corrupt.[11]

Despite some important changes beginning with the New Deal, BIA policy continued to be essentially unresponsive to those they governed through the 1960s, when the AJSS, following the well-worn path of the AFSC, first sent work campers to reservations. By then, the BIA rarely directly "ruled"; instead, individuals were appointed to limited self-governing tribal councils on the basis of how readily they followed Interior Department policies.

Henry Kohn had attempted to establish work projects on reservations for years but had met a stone wall of resistance. By now "church" groups were looked upon with hostility, as so many sects had promised help in order to promote Christianity while discouraging tribal customs. Finally, Kohn circled around the resistance by arranging for a project on the reservation in Cherokee, North Carolina in 1963. This was the first of 17 visits to Indian reservations made by AJSS projects. The North Carolina Indians were descended from those who had hidden when the Trail of Tears pushed most of their nation to Oklahoma; their reemergence as a tribal unit had not been organized until the twentieth century. But the Cherokee reservation was one of a few actually administered by the BIA in Washington, and Kohn was able to convince officials there that the AJSS project would involve youngsters in construction work beneficial to the people without promoting a social agenda.

Bureaucratic lethargy made arrangements difficult. Despite numerous phone calls cots were not located until the day before the group was to arrive, and these actually were shipped from the BIA offices in Washington. The contingent finally took up residence in a tribal town hall in Cherokee, North Carolina, in living arrangements that Kohn characterized as among the most undesirable in the history of the organization. Ed and Annette Cohen and their children were separated from the girls by hanging sheets; the boys slept in a tent behind the building.[12]

From the standpoint of the BIA and of the AJSS the work itself seemed vitally important. The reservation was without modern plumbing; local families found water aplenty in the Smoky Mountain region that was home to the reservation and would fill indoor sinks with water carried in pots.

Supervised by staff members of the United States Public Health Service, campers produced water for the homes by learning to cultivate a spring, building a concrete conduit to catch water and digging 3 foot deep trenches in rocky soil into a reservoir 6' X 8' X 12'. They dug trenches from the reservoirs to the homes, sometimes through forests, having to displace snakes and roots. The work needed the cooperation of the Indians, who gave off the distinct impression that they were humoring the BIA. The convenience of indoor plumbing was not seen as a necessity because the water was already available directly outside. This was the first example of a cultural clash that would be present at many reservation projects: what AJSS directors and campers saw as progress would not necessarily be viewed as positive by those they had come to help.

The North Carolina Cherokee had intermarried frequently with mountain people; their culture was a mixture of passed-on Indian traditions and fiddle music, which the campers heard at many dinners AJSS hosted for local residents. A medicine man came and explained how he used herbal medicine, but he admitted that if his herbs did not work when he was sick he went to a medical doctor. AJSS campers understood that they were living amidst a culture that was alien to them, but they had little sense of its overall worldview. They were, however, exposed to Cherokee history. Travelling to a tourist village, they visited a museum which detailed the Trail of Tears and saw the 50 character alphabet one of the chiefs had constructed – the first written language created in North America.[13]

Camper Stanley Herr reflected on his experience in a letter to Henry Kohn:

> It has only been a week since I have been home and in an atmosphere removed from my recent environment, yet fresh enough not to have my observations clouded by nostalgia, and I have been appraising the worth of my seven week stay in Cherokee. This summer has been an outstanding one for me, especially in regard to the work and the people it brought us into contact with, and to the impetus it has given me to delve into Jewish heritage sources and reassess my commitment to Judaism.
>
> Our accomplishments in the construction of water systems may on paper seem insignificant, but I am satisfied by the knowledge that we have advanced this work by months in excess of what the Public Health and contributing labor might have done without our assistance.
>
> But what I recall the strongest is the memory of the people we aided: simple, dignified and deeply religious people who warmed us with their gratitude and sometimes even with their love. I shall not forget the last day spent by our work group at the home of a kindly old woman on whose system we had been working for two weeks, during which time we had come to admire and become quite fond of this lady. During this period she had always treated us like her children, commenting on my underfed condition and trying to remedy it by supplementing our mid-day meal with corn, biscuits and prodigious quantities of cool-aid, telling us not to work so hard and advising us to

lie down on her sofa or bed during lunch hour, filthy blue jeans or no. The lunch she prepared on this final day was a veritable feast: heaping quantities of chicken, all the accessories, chocolate cake and ice cream. On our leaving, she wept as she kissed us all goodbye, gave each of us two jars of preserves, and to me a set of hand woven potholders for my mother. It is needless to say that we were all deeply touched by this outpouring of affection.[14]

Once one tribe had accepted an AJSS contingent, the word spread quickly along the "Moccasin Trail." The summer of 1963 saw two more reservation projects, both of them with the Oglala Sioux in South Dakota. A previously scheduled project had fallen through and two AJSS groupings lived together while working on different parts of the reservation.

Elly and Ruth Saltzman's crew worked on rebuilding a fence and constructing outdoor fireplaces for the use of tourists; Jules and Julianne Hirsh's contingent built three cabins for a school. There, the greatest impact was made by C.D. Allen, a white man hired by the BIA to be the supervisor. He impressed the campers because he shared little of the hostility and contempt for the Sioux that seemed to dominate the feelings of white South Dakotans. He was a model of efficiency and industriousness as compared to the BIA administrators, dismissed by the Hirshes with one exception as being "too concerned with their individual duties to have any concern for our needs and activities."[15]

The BIA had not prepared for the arrival of the two groups. Despite promising to arrange transportation, bureaucrats created a maze of red tape Jules had to cut through to use the empty government buses. Nor was the arrival of the AJSS broadcast to the tribes. The people seemed either indifferent or hostile. The Hirshes noted in their report, "The Indians did not know why we were there and some of those who did could not understand why teenagers from the east would pay to work on the reservation. The members of the Tribal Council did not seem to spread the news to their districts."[16] Volunteers saw written signs and heard chants of "White Trash Go Home."[17] Campers did establish good relations with the teenagers who worked at the Oglala camp; this was the main contact with the Indians.

The Saltzmans and the Hirshes were invited to a Yaweepie Ceremony in the middle of the night. They were led far away from their residence into an unlit field; for a few minutes they were surrounded by silent darkness. Suddenly a deeply felt religious ceremony, including dancing and chants began; the four AJSS project directors were stunned by the intensity of the ritual and honored to have been invited. The campers went to a commercial Sun Dance held for the benefit of tourists. The impact of the two events could not have been more different.[18]

The South Dakota plains are hot and dry and amenable to little except grain production and cattle grazing. Once, white men considered this land unattractive; maps of Indian lands in the mid-nineteenth century encompass virtually all of the state. The Oglala and Lakota tribes, first called Sioux by Indian enemies, were chased by federal troops into South Dakota from areas of Minnesota and further east. The so-called Sioux adapted to a nomadic, hunting lifestyle. Much of our muddled conception of the spiritual connection between the Indian and his prey comes from the Sioux's relationship to the buffalo.

By the late nineteenth century, the expansion of railroad lines and the discovery of mineral wealth – oil, natural gas, metals (eventually including uranium) – made the land attractive again. The government proceeded on two tracks. First, it encouraged the wholesale destruction of the buffalo to reduce the independence of the tribes; federal troops protected trains filled with rifle-toting passengers who slaughtered bison and left them to rot on the prairie. Now, desperately needed rations of flour and lard were made available only to those who would cooperate with the BIA. The very notion of the reservation came under attack by Senator Henry L. Dawes who attacked Indian life as "communism... There is no selfishness, which is at the bottom of civilization."[19]

President Benjamin Harrison grew tired of negotiating with Red Cloud and Sitting Bull; when they refused to alter earlier treaty provisions defining borders, the government simply expropriated the land and unilaterally created the reservation boundaries that now exist. Eventually Sitting Bull, who acidly noted that for whites, "the law of possessions is a disease" would be killed in a government camp he entered under the white flag of negotiation.[20]

It was in this context that the slaying of 200 occurred at Wounded Knee. A 70-year period of resigned poverty produced a culture of despair. Historian Peter Matthiessen writes, "The Lakota were forbidden the spiritual renewal of traditional ceremonies; even the ritual purification of the sweat lodge was forbidden. They were not permitted to wear Indian dress of sewn bead work, their children were seized and taken away to government boarding schools at the Pine Ridge Agency, and the use of their own language was discouraged. They were, however, invited to celebrate American Independence Day of the Fourth of July." – they turned the latter into a "secret memorial to Wounded Knee."[21]

After World War I, barter was eliminated and the tribe placed on a diet of government rations. Enterprising white people built liquor stores on the outskirts of the South Dakota reservations.[22] The legacy of bitterness and despair undoubtedly produced the hostility and indifference noticed by the Salzmans and Hirshes.

Ed and Annette Cohen's campers worked on improvements to a tourist park outside another South Dakota reservation the following summer. The work seemed tangential to the lives of the Sioux, but the campers were offered a grim education in the culture of hopelessness.

At the Rosebud reservation, people had a life expectancy of 40-45. There was high incidence of tuberculosis; campers noticed many locals had teeth rotting from cola consumption. On Saturday night, when many men would spend all their money in a local Nebraska liquor store, the Cohens were warned not to drive anywhere because of ubiquitous drunken driving.

AJSS campers lived in a mammoth school dormitory from an abandoned old boarding school. There were two or three enormous buildings of four stories each, scores of shower heads in the basement, and room after room of bunk beds on the upper floors. The vastness of the buildings made the campers feel the inhumane sting of forced "Americanization." Campers wandered through the empty structures remembering that in these classrooms, young people were punished for speaking Sioux by being hit on the hands by their teachers. Cohen ruefully comments that this was "ethnic cleansing, Indian style."[23]

AJSS campers heard these personal tales from their cook and the carpentry work supervisors. One image burnished forever in Cohen's mind was of the school building in June surrounded by hundreds of tents as parents journeyed long distances and tearfully congregated to collect their children.

A frightening education in poverty occurred the weekend the crew toured the nearby town of Spring Creek, with a population of about 1000. The village was dominated by a massive church with spires, built with Indian labor at the turn of the century under the supervision of the Catholic Church. Now only a handful of people came to mass. The builders cut down every tree to make that church; Spring Creek was now virtually barren of mature vegetation. The town had 100% unemployment. Families lived in hundreds of corrugated metal chicken coops with rounded six-foot high ceilings. The houses, all ten feet long, had dirt floors and no electricity. In the middle of the settlement stood a modern elementary school. The principal drove through the community each morning to awaken the enrolled students. During the winter he would have to eject his students at the end of the school day because his building was the only one in town with heat. [24]

In the 1960s, as the civil rights movement transformed the American south and the nation's consciousness, rumblings were heard on the reservations. Though they began elsewhere, notably in confrontations between tribes in Oregon and Washington State over fishing and water rights,[25] a ceremonial cross continental Trail of Broken treaties from Washington State to BIA headquarters in the capital helped to create a national movement.

The hottest action occurred in South Dakota during the late 1960s and early 1970s. Entrenched tribal council leadership was challenged by the new American Indian Movement. The conflict became dangerous and deadly. Although AIM members suffered the greatest casualties, they were the ones arrested for violent crimes by the FBI. A ceremonial sit-in at Wounded Knee led to a prolonged stand-off between the G-men and AIM.

Though neither faction was able to maintain power, renewed cultural rituals were established. During the mid-1970s, morale rose for a time. Both South Dakota senators, including 1972 Presidential candidate George McGovern, became vocal advocates for local autonomy and empowerment. When Carl and Audrey Brenner brought a crew to renovate an old Civilian Conservation Corps campsite and restore the oldest Christian-Indian cemetery on the Sisseton-Wahpeton Sioux Reservation, they were warmly welcomed. Senator McGovern spent time conversing with each member of the crew and toured the worksite.[26]

The way the group touched one local resident was perhaps more memorable. David Weber of the Northeast South Dakota Community Action Program, which hosted the project, wrote,

> I must tell you about an incident which will show you further the impact which AJSS had here.
>
> Sisseton is finally coming under a long neglected scrutiny for its incredible racism and prejudice. There was a large meeting here of local and state employment people, and Etta Finley was asked to speak. For the first time in her 68 years here on the reservation she was speaking out, in public, on prejudice. This act was for her, let me assure you, awesome. She at first seemed at a loss for words. Then she began telling about this summer, when we had a group of white Jewish people here. Whenever they saw her on the street, she told the audience, they would run up to her, grab her, touch her, talk to her. Never before had there been a group of white teenagers in Sisserton who gave a damn whether she was on the street or not. Because this memory made her feel so good, she went on to give a moving, sad and happy speech.[27]

Sadly, the mass impoverishment and lack of a viable economy there has led to little change in the hopelessness on the Dakota reservations, as Marty and Rochelle Kopelowitz discovered when they led a group to the Crow Creek Sioux Reservation, southeast of Pierre. The project itself was testimony to the problem, as the contingent was asked to renovate the Swift House Lodge which housed an alcoholic rehabilitation program.

The reservation was particularly isolated, being fifty miles to Pierre and fifty miles to tiny Chamberlain, a town of two blocks. Rochelle Kopelowitz, a veteran of 27 AJSS summers, remembers that it contained, "the poorest people I've ever seen." The women appeared the most run-down. "If they were 30, they looked 60." The barrenness seemed surreal: there was no work, no industry, no visible natural resources and dry, brown soil.

After they first arrived, AJSS volunteers painted the Alcohol Rehabilitation Center inside and out; the crew got to know people living there. When this work was completed, painting continued, this time of a community center, which housed a liquor store because of the tribal leadership's desire to cut down on drunk driving deaths. People seen in the rehab facility two weeks earlier were now begging money to buy alcohol inside the community center.

Education of another sort occurred after a game of flag football. When the group repaired to its quarters to clean up, they found it surrounded by rattlesnakes. The football players stayed sweaty until the snakes crawled away.

Invited to two powwows by Swift House Lodge Director Clark Zephier, who had previously detailed the history of the tribe, the crew was "thrilled by the beauty of the dress, the magnificence of the dancing, and the uniqueness of the drum and song."[28] AJSS volunteered to serve dinner; in addition to other food, campers baked and served challah. The weather-beaten faces in Indian costumes left indelible images in campers' minds.[29] Still, more than one camper found Indian teenagers and children friendly and receptive, though one opined that the alcoholism was "shocking and saddening."[30]

Though reservation life is never luxurious, AJSS campers have found situations sharply divergent from the despairing impoverishment of South Dakota. One summer after Pine Ridge, Jules and Julianne Hirsh brought a crew to work with the Chippewa tribe in Cloquet, Minnesota. The work featured demolition of the front of an unused federal Indian hospital and beginning the building's transformation into a community center. Though some on the reservation were indifferent to the work, tribal leaders and work supervisors indigenous to the reservation were effusive about its importance. Of more significance to the campers, "Various teenage boys and girls would come and work all day with our group." Adults watched, and occasionally one would spend a day off of work working with our group. "Early one morning our group arrived at the project to find a man working alone on the roof. By the middle of the afternoon he single-handedly removed a large section of roof and left." Women often brought coffee and donuts. "One of the teenage girls, Bonnie Wallace, had her mother make a small birch bark canoe as a gift for each camper."[31]

Artie Mayer, one of the volunteers, was appreciative of the personal interaction. After the summer, he wrote to Henry Kohn,

> Towards the end of the summer more and more new Indian faces came out to work with us at the project. In a way, this showed their acceptance of us. It also showed their gratefulness. It is a much better feeling to work with the Indian when both of you really care what you're doing than when you're working for him without his realizing that you want to help and his not caring about what you're doing.
>
> What this nation and this world need is more people who really care about their fellow man and are willing to do something to improve humanity. Then the world would be a much better place in which to live.[32]

Carl and Audrey Brenner got a sudden education in an alien world when they were hired in June 1968 as emergency replacements after Ed Cohen's heart attack ended his tenure as a project director. With no time for their own preliminary visit of Crow Agency, Montana, the Brenners made use of Cohen's slides at orientation. Making swift arrangements for recreation for their sons (ages 9, 7, 5), the novice directors placed them in a day camp with local youngsters, only to find them in tears after they were taunted with shouts of "Blue Eyes Go Home." The Brenner boys do not have blue eyes. Much to the Brenners' surprise, the hostility expressed by the Indians toward the Brenner children was sympathized with by the AJSS campers because they saw the Indians as oppressed.

The campers were perhaps too representative of their times. On the second day, the Brenners remember, "Out comes the pot." At 11 PM the reservation police reported conversations between AJSS kids and local teens about their marijuana possession; Carl confronted his group and flushed the cannabis down the toilet.

The previous summer an AFSC project at Crow Agency had been disastrous; the college volunteers had not performed up to expectations, so there was some initial suspicion of the AJSS group. The work supervisor was the local sheriff and gas station owner, Mark Small. He was not prepared for the contingent's arrival. The first week of work was garbage pick-up and then the building of a cemetery fence. The volunteers were at first troubled by the insubstantial work they were offered; picking up garbage others idly tossed away was particularly troublesome. "The main thing the kids learned was that we did what they [the Indian project hosts] thought was important. This showed that we were there to help them." The campers learned not to judge Indians' priorities, but many could not help questioning. Around them, filthy homes all had televisions and meat hung out to dry, sometimes off of TV antennas.

One camper expressed her dilemma this way:

> What am I doing here? Why am I digging post holes and painting fences? Why do I get up early every morning to work in the hot sun or under the dark clouds? Did I come here to build a fence or was I dreaming of glory? Did I want to single-handedly heal the wounds of the Indian people? How can I free myself of guilt I did not earn? Why was I born white?[34]

Still, the summer proved successful. When the tribe saw the completed fence, it was happy to ask for additional work. Pulling unused railroad stakes out of the ground to reclaim lumber, volunteers stockpiled the wood to build a racetrack. Of course, the campers would have preferred building homes. Instead they created a half-mile oval racetrack, using survey techniques to map it as they planned the racetrack on graph paper and marked the area with string. Campers were asked to understand that the tourist money anticipated from the race track would benefit the whole tribe. Additional projects included picnic tables for tourist stops and ditch digging for individual garbage disposals. One moment was cherished by camper Larry Green, who felt delighted to discover that while the AJSS contingent ate lunch, local children continued the hole digging for the garbage disposal. "This had been our goal: to involve the Indians in our work."[35]

Three weeks after the group's arrival it was invited to an Indian Powwow in Lane Deer in its honor; the full dress was scary in the pitch dark. After watching the Indian dancing, AJSS volunteers demonstrated a hora.

News of the Brenners' work in Montana spread 50 miles east and the Crow agency invited the AJSS back, this time to work under the direction of Jules and Julianne Hirsh. The population on the reservation was under 2000; the few whites worked for the government. Despite the annual commemoration of Custer's Last Stand with the white town of Hardin, there was no cooperation during the year. Only two Indians were employed in the whole town, where residents expressed open, ugly prejudice against the Crows.

The Brenner group would have been gratified by the nature of the work. Forty three-bedroom homes available for small cost and sweat equity were being offered to tribe members. AJSS worked on a variety of construction tasks on these homes. The first 11 families moved in (after two years of work) during the 1969 summer. Naturally enough, the AJSS contingent felt a "tremendous morale boost" in seeing the families ensconced in their new habitats.

None of the hostility of the previous year was in evidence. The Hirshes wrote of a warm relationship throughout the summer. Campers attended a Crow celebration and all were given an "authentic beaded necklace or bolo tie." The contingent played weekly baseball games with Indian teens. "In previous years we had a good relationship with the leaders but not with the Indian community in general as we did this year." Jules arranged speakers on Crow history, folklore, culture, and social problems.

One disturbing feature of the previous stay re-emerged: Two traveling college students supplied three AJSS volunteers with marijuana, and they gave it to Indian teens. Other visitors isolated the two college students, threatening them with arrest. Jules and Julianne Hirsh led an impromptu education seminar on the perils of drugs. Even dangerous situations have their upside: AJSS campers in two successive summers were forced to contrast contemporary mores about drugs with the problems of alcoholism on the reservation.[36]

During the late 1960s and 1970s, it was not unnatural for students to associate Indians with hallucinogens. Sun dances and peyote are acclaimed for achieving a mind-changing spirituality; Indians were being celebrated for achieving a mindset that rejected the crass materialism student leaders connected to the Vietnam war.

Indeed project directors who directed groups at the height of student dissent and also decades later found the earlier groups to be more difficult – and more rewarding. More defiant of authority, more likely to smuggle marijuana or alcohol, they were also more likely to be reflective social critics, to link their AJSS summers to notions of societal transformation.[37]

The Hirshes' thoughtful counselor, Arthur Janovsky, probed Joe Ten Bear on the future of his tribe. The tribal secretary was not sanguine, believing that "the Crow Culture had been destroyed beyond any hope of complete revival; in fact such a revival would be unrealistic in view of the world of today."[38]

The hostility and prejudice separating whites from Indians so prevalent in South Dakota and Montana was absent in Cloquet, Minnesota. As in Abbeville, Louisiana, the AJSS crew provided a model for the neighboring white community; some locals admitted to the Hirshes that "they never knew how to attempt to help the Indians and that it was sometimes easier for an outside group to start the ball rolling." A shop teacher stopped by to observe the work, saw his former students, and wound up advising and working with the AJSS to put up the roof. In a casual conversation in Cloquet, Jules found an electrician when one was needed. The Presbyterian Youth Fellowship saw a newspaper article about the Jewish teenagers in a local paper; they invited the AJSS group to a cookout and picnic and one girl worked most of the last two weeks, sometimes bringing friends with her to work as well.[39] When the summer was over Cloquet teenager Christina Gullion wrote to Jules Hirsh:

> In the few contacts I had with you, I learned how foolish prejudice can be and how shallow ignorance is.
> Meeting all of you made me realize how close all mankind can be, and made me realize that religion is but a shallow barrier, that inside – in the heart and soul – the different religious teachings are basically the same and can live side by side in harmony and for the betterment of all men.
> The presence of AJSS also gave me the opportunity to work for people for whom I had never before had compassion. Through working at the new community center I saw that Indians are *people*, not just a deprived and needy race which deserved a better break. Thank you for this new insight.[40]

Two AJSS projects on Navajo reservations left indelible images in the minds of campers more powerful than any formal education experience. In Steamboat Canyon, Arizona, the volunteers struggled with frustration as "sporadic" work supervision delayed their project of installing new sewer lines at Steamboat Canyon School, which trained adults in employment skills. The job was successfully completed, and campers also served as assistant teachers in the school. The contingent toured Mesa Verde and the Grand Canyon on weekends.[41] Becky Srole vividly recorded her impressions in the project newsletter, "The Pipeline":

> I saw a girl with matted hair, crusty nose, and fear in her eyes.
> I saw the endless ceiling of sky as a billion stars warmed the dead silence.
> I saw miles of land baking in the sun – red and lonely.
> I saw a tiny brown baby strapped on a cradleboard held by his sister.
> I heard the sound of children's laughter as a starving dog searched the ground.
> I saw a gnarled old woman cry at a Mormon pageant.
> I saw slices of great canyons cut by hungry nature.
> I saw a class of grown men smile as the Constitution was recited.
> I saw a long string of telephone poles holding secrets no one knows.

I saw a young girl rattle a cup at her sheep herd.
I saw a man with a hook-hand read through a first grade primer.
I saw gray gulches where rivers once flowed.
I saw the sun rise over a wonder of the world.
I saw huge clouds of dust rolling in the hot wind.
I saw scuffed, worn boots radiating past glories.
I saw dark, empty faces approach a blue-eyed trader.
I saw the beauty of the land reflected in human faces.
                    Ha gona sik is
                    Good-bye, my brother[42]

Two years earlier, in Crownpoint, New Mexico, campers improved a local recreation area by demolishing several structures, landscaping the area, erecting a mile of barbed wire fence, and building sun shelters. They also engaged in several smaller construction jobs in town.[43] But the most memorable moment of the summer took place off of the worksite. Camper Alice Fay wrote:

> Perhaps one of my most vivid memories of AJSS in Crownpoint is the time we went to a sheep slaughtering at the Mescal farm. I can still picture the scene: Mrs. Mescal quietly and elegantly sawing through the windpipe, the doomed animal bound and squirming on a ripped-open cardboard box; her daughter gently but firmly holding it down, directly surrounded by 20-odd panting, poking, Jewish work campers, counselors, director and family, horrified and wholly fascinated. Then I see the shed, one-half enclosing the operation, the compact home across from it and a little further in the distance the pen filled with noisy sheep not yet touched by the hand of fate. And when it was all over, the insides taken out, commented on and washed, and the mutton was on the fire, sizzling like any other piece of meat, it was hard to believe that what we had seen had really taken place. But, as we sat in the shed munching alternately bites of mutton roast, stew and fry bread, (especially Joe's Fry Bread Challah) occasionally bumping our heads on the sheep's insides neatly strung up in the shed to dry, the idea that I had known the sheep when it was alive came back to me, and I couldn't eat another bite. Then I started to think why I was nauseous. After all, this was their way of life and we were lucky enough to have the chance to observe it. Besides, they would probably be twice as nauseated by the Lexington IRT subway. But the whole value of the experience is not only that it showed How Navajos Live, but that we learned that whatever is necessary to a man is sacred and far above the reach of petty emotion. And then I remembered another thing. When she finally finished cutting and stripping the flesh off the prone sheep, Mrs. Mescal didn't have to wipe her hands – they were completely clean.[44]

Another camper, Ruth Obernbreit, reacted this way:

> I saw the head lying there and objectively knew that plants live off other plants, animals live off plants and other animals and we too, in order to survive we must kill. But I subjectively saw the sheep's head, and it looked human. I recalled the countless pictures of slaughtering in Nazi concentration camps, and stories of relatives I've never met done away with in the same fashion, as nonchalantly. I attempted to stop the association but felt the nausea in my throat and tears in my eyes and I had to turn away.[45]

Two other teenagers were powerfully affected by a stomp dance they attended. Andrea Edson and Patti-Lou Schultz wrote:

> People, the majority of whom were Indians, began moving back and forth, their bodies swaying to the rhythm. Sweat fell from their bodies and faces. It was a dizzy kaleidoscope of sounds... I stood up and with another member of the group started to sway with the music. Trying to look as inconspicuous as possible, I attempted to do a modified skate. I hung my head down, afraid to look up. But finally my will power could stand it no more. Sure enough, faces were aimed at my direction, eyes staring, staring, staring. I walked to the side and sat down with the rest of the group who were also suffering from shock and were trembling quite violently. At 11:15 finally, the man with the camera [Jules Hirsh] came and took us away. We went out into the cool air, visions of the night remaining in our heads for a long time to come.[46]

The volunteers in Crownpoint felt the profundity of an alien culture with which they sympathized and longed to understand. Nonetheless, there are clear limits. Unlike the black churches in the south, where AJSS campers have been welcome and frequently honored, the sacredness of Indian ritual includes a wariness of outsiders which defies ready penetration. Though individual groups have been invited, most often they have been spectators, aware that they have witnessed a moving emotional experience they cannot fully articulate.

One of the differences between reservation life and impoverishment in the black south is physical. Abbeville, Louisiana, Clinton, Kentucky, or Selma, Alabama are bounded by village or township lines. There are community centers where active churches, schools, and stores unify many residents and provide a common pulse whose beat can be heard or felt by visitors. Reservations in the west, as I learned on my orientation trip to Wyoming in 1998, are first memorable for their undifferentiated vastness.

Schooled by western movies and television programs, I was expecting a recognizable entranceway, perhaps a wooden Disneyland frontier town surrounded by teepees. Instead, driving west from Casper on US Highway 26, I discovered that the small metal highway sign reading "Wind River Indian Reservation" denoted absolutely no change in the landscape. Identical fields of sagebrush and oddly sculpted rock hosting clusters of antelope under an endless horizon presented themselves on both sides of the sign.

Riverton, a population center of 10,000, was carved out of the reservation when settlers arrived from the East. Though it is surrounded by tribal land, it is not part of the reservation, and it is essentially identical to thousands of small American towns. The traveler enters after passing through a couple of miles of fast food outlets and strip malls. Wal-Mart is the busiest of the stores. The old downtown, including a couple of establishments offering local beadwork, is five or six blocks long; uptown, the high school and college campus proudly display modern design and ample space for expansion. In another mile, the visitor is again back on the open spaces of the reservation, instantly becoming more magnificent with each passing mile as the Wind River Mountains – the Wyoming Rockies – climb toward the continental divide.

Turn onto a smaller road leading to scattered houses on the reservation; the changes are subtle but produce a growing sense of isolation. In addition to tracts of tumbleweeds and grazing land, the plateau includes many acres of undisciplined greenery - weeds and grain gone to seed at waist level. Even a functioning mineral processing plant near Riverton is surrounded in this way by undomesticated nature. Scattered throughout are abandoned, rusty cars and domiciles of all types. Though some are newly built and seem more than adequate, their haphazard placement and the absence of landscaping unites them with the scores of dilapidated trailers. A single trailer might be surrounded by four or five old cars, testimony to a score of residents cramped inside. Stretching over two million acres, the reservation includes tiny settlements of two or three stores and an occasional gas station, school, church, community center, graveyard, and even a nursing home.

Wind River County Habitat for Humanity employed AJSS in the construction of one unusual house on the reservation. Housed in St. John's Lutheran Church in Riverton, the group traveled ten minutes to the worksite, the last two minutes on a dirt road, to work on the newly born Habitat chapter's second house.

> And what a house! Though following a typical Habitat footprint for a three bedroom home, Mike and Laura Lee Monroe's castle is an experiment. This is a straw bale house. After the beer companies harvest the barley crop, the resulting straw is too tough for animal feed, but baled, it represents a phenomenal natural insulator. The thick bale walls are stuccoed, creating the ideal house to confront rough Wyoming winters and winds. For four weeks we worked on the Monroe house, installing windows and soffets, affixing and sewing chicken wire to the bales for the stucco to adhere to, and sheetrocking and taping the interior walls.[47]

The AJSS contingent learned a great deal about bale houses. Volunteers toured the first completed straw house in the area and heard agricultural experts explain how the work benefited home owners and farmers alike. Much more significant was the cultural education made available to the crew.

The Wind River Reservation is home to two tribes, the Shoshone and the Arapaho. That decision was made in Washington, after federal officials decided to uproot the Arapaho from lands south. There is an uneasy peace between the two, and our project did not result in much contact with the Shoshone nation. But two factors enabled the AJSS contingent to feel personally welcomed by members of the Arapaho tribe.

A lucky coincidence placed our program nearby the summer home of Rabbi Harry Levin, a 1971 AJSS camper. Levin adopted the group as his responsibility during its stay on the reservation. His self-imposed responsibilities as a host were varied, but perhaps his most significant contribution occurred when he brought young tribal leader Allison Sage to speak about his people's culture and history. Sage concluded his remarks by teaching the group dances and chants to the accompaniment of his drum.

Young home owners Mike and Laura Monroe made the most significant contribution to the contingent's understanding. Dedicated, intelligent, and forthright, the Monroes are a remarkable couple. Laura has refused to make the cerebral palsy which keeps her on crutches a handicap. After traveling to Montana to earn her masters degree in social work, Laura elected to return to the reservation to found a center for abused women and children. She seeks to spearhead an active role in educating her people about alcoholism and spousal and child abuse. She spent an evening discussing the social problems on the reservation and her undying commitment to defeating the social ills which hurt those who live there. Laura also arranged a tour of the Catholic center on the reservation, and she and Mike noted the church's use of Indian symbols to subvert the tribal religion which created them. Wind River Habitat Director Cathy Yoccheim emphasized Laura's steely resolve. Mrs. Monroe stood still on her crutches at the tribal council meeting until the leadership moved beyond partisan bickering with the Shoshone and approved the construction of her home.

Mike also had an opportunity to leave the reservation. Blessed with musical talent, he was awarded a full scholarship to the Julliard School in Manhattan following high school. But the reservation, for all its problems, meant home and ties to identity; Mike turned the scholarship down. He and Laura decided to remain with their nation because they are convinced their children must grow up with a sense of their identity. Normally a travelling fire fighter, one who volunteers for the emergency blazes that make the national news, Mike became the work supervisor on his own house, and his daily contact with the volunteers was their most significant learning experience. Mike was able with his hands, and he was fine in helping to organize and direct the group. But more important were his direct honesty, his calm manner, and the quiet earnestness which is his code in life. The group had been invited to a sun dance, but Mike stressed that this ritual should not be a tourist attraction; instead it is the most strenuous attempt by members of the nation to commune with their gods. No one would prevent us from going, but while we would be tolerated, we would be intruding on the solemnity of the occasion. The crew did not attend.

Instead Mike spent lunch breaks teaching tribal games and song. He and his brother also brought drums and instructed the group in chant and dance. His informal discussion of his people's mores, such as the innate generosity which is part of their customs (if someone warmly appreciates an object of another, the second person will make a gift of it), gave the campers an understanding no history or formal presentation could have approached.

Of course personal relationships are the basis for much significant learning. Though AJSS campers cannot fathom the total experience, they can, by working and living side by side with people like Mike Monroe, begin to bridge the gulf which makes strangers of easterners and westerners, suburbanites and reservation dwellers, Jews and Indians, lost tribes searching for a renewed identity.

Henry Kohn and Sister Anne Catherine Bizalion in Abbeville, Louisiana in 1971. The AJSS and Sister Anne's organization, the Southern Mutual Help Association, collaborated on four projects of great significance to both groups.

In 1963, the AJSS sent all three projects to Indian reservations, the beginning of an important tradition. Elly and Ruth Saltzman are in the lower left with their Pine Ridge, South Dakota contingent.

Project director Ed Cohen speaks to camper-roofers in Palatine, Illinois in 1965.

Two generations of project directors pose with the group in Seaford, Delaware in 1970. Jules Hirsh is third from the left on the ground. Sitting on the truck's side is Julianne and their two young children. Jonathan, absorbing future leadership tips, smiles and squints at the camera.

Carl and Audrey Brenner stand at the right with their Las Cruces, New Mexico contingent in 1977. Camper Fred Nathan is in the top row, third from the left.

The AJSS has built many roofs. This representative photo was snapped in Hattiesburg, Mississippi in 1978.

Alone among the three founding rabbis, Isidor Hoffman made annual visits to the projects during the first 30 years. Here he removes nails in North Carolina.

Camper Rena Convissor nails under the watchful eyes of a work supervisor in Jeanerette, Louisiana, site of the 1980 work with the Southern Mutual Help Association.

Sarah Lytle installs insulation on the first AJSS project sponsored by Habitat for Humanity. Amarillo, Texas, 1985.

Rochelle and Marty Kopelowitz stand with their 1990 Detroit group. Campers contributed valuable labor and experienced frightening- and educational -inner-city tension.

Campers constructing the community center in Four Corners Louisiana which Hurricane Andrew would topple several weeks later in 1992. Under SMHA leadership, the community rebuilt it.

The author at work with his first AJSS grouping, demolishing an old house in Selma, Alabama before the construction of a Habitat home in 1993.

A Jewish education sometimes includes opening a synagogue which is normally closed except for the High Holy Days. Camper David Alima blows the shofar in Presque Isle, Maine's temple in 1995.

The construction of the Double Vee Monument in the Victory Over Violence Park marked an AJSS contribution to symbolic healing in Milwaukee in 1997. Jonathan Hirsh kneels in front of Karin Kaiser who is holding the youngest of their three children.

Roof construction in Escanaba, Michigan in 1999.

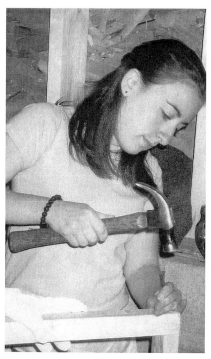

Sara Pflantzer creates a wall section in Marquette, Michigan, 1999.

AJSS trips explore the beauty of the nation. The 1994 Phoenix group with the Grand Canyon behind them.

The Grand Tetons frame the 2000 Riverton, Wyoming contingent.

White Water Rafting is a favorite activity for weekend recreation. Here the 2000 Montana campers brave the river.

Henry Kohn with the US map displaying fifty years and 121 AJSS projects.

The author and his wife Catherine atop a Wyoming Butte in 1998.

5

The Many Faces of Poverty

When the American Jewish Society for Service was founded, its direction ran counter to the main movement of American society. Five years into the post-war boom, depression and starving masses seemed relics of the past. Still, difficulties remained. Real estate developers could not keep pace with the housing shortage; migration out of the south and the Appalachian coal fields kept cities of the northeast, midwest, and increasingly the west expanding with prospective new employees. But as the decade progressed, most Americans benefited from the remarkable expansion of the American economy, as "between 1949 and 1960 absolute real Gross National Product increased from over $206 billion to over $500 billion, a rise of nearly 51 percent."[1]

Among the new growth industries was television, which after a loving look back at past models of inner city working class families – *The Honeymooners, I Remember Mama, The Goldbergs* – adopted the ideal of suburban tranquility in such shows as *Father Knows Best* and *The Donna Reed Show*. Though only two decades removed from the end of the great depression, most Americans thought of their nation as contentedly prosperous, with New Deal social programs enveloping all in protection against scarcity and want.

Thus the culture of national abundance was far more ubiquitous than plenty itself. As early as 1958 economist John Kenneth Galbraith warned *The Affluent Society* that the emergence of a middle class majority was blinding the nation to many who had been left behind as the good ship prosperity cruised the American ocean.[2]

The young people working on AJSS projects could have provided several case studies. Whether working with veterans to erase slums in Indianapolis or working in the northeast, the south and the midwest to improve recreation facilities for inner city youngsters, AJSS volunteers addressed persistent poverty in the land.

Campers in 1960 traveled to Buckhorn, Kentucky to build a school gymnasium for an orphanage in the Cumberland Mountains. As coal mining was eliminated, the poor farming community that remained behind did not have the funds to pay contractors to complete the work; the Presbyterian Child Welfare

Agency sought AJSS aid. Counselor Barbara Hyams told the *New York Times* about the value of the experience: "It was a wonderful, heart-warming experience. Our children came from soft backgrounds, little hard work. But we learned the meaning of work, the meaning of religious and cultural understanding."[3] They also learned, two years before the rest of the United States, that the Appalachian region, ironically the focus of intensive American Friends Service Committee attention during the depression, was being squeezed by the contraction of the two arenas which had been the backbone of life in the area: the farms and coal fields.

Michael Harrington graphically reminded the nation that the prosperous façade of America concealed 40 to 50 million people living in poverty. *The Other America* described them as "invisible: they live in unseen slums or in rural areas; they're black, they're old, they're young, they're migrants. They dress just like everyone else. Over eight million are over 65. More are under 18. They are politically powerless, having no advocates."[4]

Noting the varied face of poverty, Harrington described the conditions in the rural east. "They live in the Appalachian Mountains where mining has left and the hills make farming impossibly labor intensive in the face of mechanized agriculture." Miners who worked for 19 years did not leave when the mines closed, hoping futilely to get their jobs back to qualify for a pension.[5] Nor was farming a logical alternative:

> According to the US Dept of Agriculture, the average investment per farm increased some six times between 1940 and 1959. The amount of working hours spent on food production has been in almost steady decline since the end of World War I (and right after World War II the average dropped by 700,000,000 man hours a year). As a result, there has been a decline of almost 2,000,000 units in the number of farms since 1930.[6]

Many who remained in farming were black. Deborah Sharpe, a thoughtful camper who accompanied the Brenners to Ripley, Tennessee in 1969, gave theoretical perspective to her experience in a reflection that reads like an appendix to Harrington's national best seller:

> As a "Northerner," I guess I had always felt some sort of satisfaction that it was the North who freed the slaves, and "saved" the South from "inevitable self-destruction." But what a fallacy. I had never before fully realized what had happened to thousands of poor Whites and Blacks as a result of the Civil War. Slavery was bad, but I now realize that we have replaced slavery with a system which is not much better. The sharecropper- tenant farmer system that exists today is frightening. I get the impression that the sharecropper is worse off in many respects than a slave ever was; for he is still a slave to the land, and tied to the landowner as well, by debt. The landowner neither has

to provide for his tenant's welfare nor for his health, for the sharecropper is not property. (One family was in threat of eviction from their shack for the landlord felt that it would be more profitable to use the shack as a hay barn.) There are so many unskilled workers available that the landowner need not worry about insufficient cheap labor. To add to the problems of the poor, industrialization of farming has enabled the wealthier landowners to buy out small farmers and to replace many former workers with machines. As a result, the people we worked for were for the most part on welfare; they did not own the land they lived on; and they lived under appalling conditions – with no running water, no sewage system, hungry and with insufficient clothing. The poor Blacks face the additional problem of racial prejudice. Their total dependence upon their White landlords seems to frighten these poor away from any form of protest – for they have everything to lose.

What was created along with emancipation and industrialization was a class system of the very rich and the very poor, with a relatively small middle or working class. (Sixty per cent of Ripley's 4,000 people are at the poverty level.) The social problems are much more complex than I ever had realized, and the government is having minimal success in its efforts to rehabilitate the area.

Food stamps do not provide food for those who cannot afford to buy the stamps. Industry is being brought into the area in an effort to employ the displaced farmers. The people most in need of work, however, are uneducated and unskilled in anything but farming. For the young, with their newly acquired education, there is little opportunity in the South and this results in a mass migration of the youth, the skilled, and the educated to the northern cities. Every family I worked with had older children in Detroit or Chicago. In all likelihood the migration will continue, for the sons write glowing reports home about the grand life in the big cities.[7]

Harrington's book created a much larger storm than Galbraith's had four years earlier. John Kennedy authorized studies to create a program, but little had been decided before his death. Kennedy advisor Walter Heller was given authority by President Johnson to devise a program. The bill that rushed through congress had many sections; historians find little evidence that Johnson had much interest in pursuing the details. Still, as with civil rights, the new chief executive proved more skilled than his predecessor in pushing liberal priorities. Historian Irving Bernstein remarks on the president's shrewdness in selecting Georgia Dixiecrat Phil Landrum to guide the program through congress. What emerged was a new series of acronyms and government bureaucracies. The Organization for Economic Opportunity was the umbrella agency overseeing the Job Corps, Volunteers In Service To America, and Head Start. From the first a local organizing component was embraced and funded.[8]

VISTA authorized individuals to use federal funds to create or strengthen local organizations attacking poverty conditions. Sometimes, as in Ripley, Tennessee where local OEO organizer Levi Moore's dynamic leadership galvanized the community and awed AJSS volunters, the organization had roots in the community;[9] sometimes, as in Clinton, Kentucky, an outsider like Mike Shapiro struggled vainly to overcome local prejudice.[10]

The War on Poverty was, with the president's commitment to civil rights, the moral centerpiece of Johnson's Great Society. Despite the later attacks on the poverty program as a symbol of out-of-control liberal spending, the money congress authorized never came close to tackling the enormity of the challenge it addressed. While the poorly organized national and state bureaucracies undoubtedly funded many incompetent and perhaps corrupt functionaries, no anti-poverty program could undertake the great task unless expenditures would match the mammoth costs of the president's other war. It never came close. The total amount appropriated to end poverty for upwards of 40 million Americans came to $1.6 billion.[11] The cost of killing two million Vietnamese and Americans during the eight years between 1965 and 1973 was $120 billion.[12]

Still, whatever its shortcomings, the poverty program marked the first time in a generation that the federal government committed itself to its neediest citizens. For the tiny American Jewish Society for Service, it meant looking for sponsorship beyond the narrow boundaries of local volunteer associations, most of them operating, as did the AJSS itself, out of a religious commitment to the needs of others.

Both OEO and VISTA proved to be vital organizational links for the AJSS. With the implementation of the Johnson poverty apparatus, the early difficulties in obtaining projects vanished. By the mid to late 1960s, initial contacts and cooperation between AJSS and OEO or VISTA were publicized in the in-house VISTA magazine, and before Henry Kohn searched for projects, local leaders contacted him. Work in Wisconsin in 1966, in Missouri in 1967, in Clinton, Kentucky in 1968, in Ripley, Tennessee in 1969 and in McAllen, Texas in 1970 were all facilitated by the new federal poverty bureaucracy.[13]

Even after the poverty organizations were largely abandoned by changed federal priorities in 1981, the skeletal network of state VISTA organizations remained the principal source for spreading the word that AJSS was available to help struggling non-profits address local conditions.

Harrington pointed out, and the OEO's varied operations demonstrated, that poverty in the United States was multi-faceted. One poor American in five, he claimed, was over 65.

How well that dovetailed with the AJSS experience! Often the organization worked on renovation projects to improve the homes of the elderly. The Oregon Hill Home Improvement Corporation of Richmond, Virginia, organized a home repair effort for an impoverished white community that drew AJSS participation in

1973. "Most of the applicants were either aged, widowed, or physically handicapped."[14]

In Clinton, Iowa, camper Felice Burstein noted, "This summer was not about construction, sightseeing, and abstracts such as poverty and altruism. It's about people: an old lady who has lived alone for years and adopted us as her own, an old man who makes necklaces and plays poker, a great grandmother who gets out and washes her windows, [and] an old lady who gets up after her stroke to look at her new porch."[15]

Several memorable black women – Mrs. Tate in Jackson, Mississippi, Mrs. Miller in Alice, Texas, Mrs. Latham, in Greenville, North Carolina, and Mrs. Wilson in Abbeville, Louisiana – were impressive for maintaining their purposefulness and faith into their old age. Project newsletters contain numerous accounts of personal reactions to old people without economic resources, struggling to maintain their dignity amid squalor. Nor was the work always welcomed by the campers.

In 1994 in Eugene, Oregon, campers worked on a variety of projects under the supervision of the Society of Saint Vincent de Paul. There the organization was active in restoring old housing and building hundreds of low-income units. For most of the summer, volunteers worked renovating housing before new owners moved in, but one assignment was memorable, if not exactly pleasant. Society social worker Eileen Purdy asked the group to aid 89 year old George Clark, restricted to movement with a walker and despondent after the death of his wife of 62 years. For three days, AJSS volunteers cleaned, removed fencing and debris, and repainted Clark's home. In doing so, they walked, both inside the house and out, through the feces of dogs and cats living with him. The greatest shock occurred outside; when clearing the yard, campers came upon the still reeking remains of a dog. In fact smell was the sense that created the most lasting memory of the experience. Throughout it all, George talked with campers and shared the experiences of his own youth. Those who worked inside and spoke with him had a more positive attitude than those who worked outside, despite the greater intensity of disagreeable odors within the house.[16]

The continuous contraction of farmland and farming jobs has been a story as old as the end of the frontier. The postwar era has included the virtual elimination of profitable small-scale farming. One camper, working in Bluffton, Ohio to repair tornado damage, memorialized this vanishing American:

> We've learned about the farmer, a sort of mystical person in N.Y.C. who supplies our milk and green beans, but someone whom we know almost nothing about. The farmer is an independent person – a proud person who trusts himself and has confidence in himself. He doesn't easily ask for the help of others but when he does he is not ashamed. At the beginning of the trip I used to ask, "Fred, can I use the saw; can I hammer in these nails?" meaning of course to ask permission.

You don't need to ask someone else; just truthfully ask yourself. The answer the farmer always gave was, "Sure, if you want to." The farmer is not too quick at praising, but when he does, he means it. I get the feeling that he won't make his judgment on whether or not you drive a spike or "20-penny" in straight.

Through the generosity and kindness of the people we've met this summer, I've acquired an increased faith in man. I've lost much of my school-year pessimism. I like the way folks smile here; they seem more genuine.[17]

More frequently AJSS projects in farm country involved the organization with tenant farmers and migrants. Historian Jacqueline Jones has summarized the larger historic trend:

Out of the devastation of the Civil War emerged a class of landless Southern families that picked the cotton that fueled the South's economic recovery. The fathers and sons from these families, men of both races, worked elbow to elbow in the steaming phosphate pits and side by side in swampland lumber camps and turpentine stills throughout the rural South. From the late nineteenth century onward, forces of the global market economy intruded into the countryside, dispossessed large numbers of Southerners of their homes and the living they wrung from the soil, and pushed them into nearby towns and, after 1916, up north or out west. Deep South black migrants joined with Appalachian white migrants in an effort to establish a foothold in Northern industry; but the declining demand for unskilled labor relegated some of the whites, and most of the blacks, to the margins of modern society. In the 1960s and 1970s automation at home and competition from abroad rendered more and more manual workers entirely superfluous within a reordered world economy. At the same time an influx of refugees from Latin America and Southeast Asia provided cheap labor for the sweatshop owners of New York City and the truck-farm employers up and down the East Coast. This process of displacement and dispersal represented a variation of larger, worldwide migrations that had affected rural folk through the centuries. By the 1990s America's internal colonial economy had grown to the point that observers likened conditions in the South Bronx, and in the hills and hollows of Appalachia, to those in the Third World.[18]

For most AJSS Project Directors, the poverty among migrant farm workers has been the most harrowing they've witnessed. Ed Cohen vividly described conditions in the Missouri Bootheel:

The Bootheel is reputed to be one of the most poverty-stricken areas of the nation. Signs of a once prosperous region are apparent. Closed cotton gins, boarded-up houses, deserted factories and movies are visible in many communities.

In the '40s and before, "cotton was king." Now with the competition of synthetic fibers and automation, cotton producers cannot even sustain the small population in the Bootheel. For this reason most able-bodied men, women, and children leave this area to earn a living picking fruit and vegetables in Ohio, Michigan, Florida, etc. While most return to their homes in the Bootheel for two to three months, they are classified as migrants. Dilapidated buses, which carry migrants and those who work in the Bootheel "choppin' cotton," are seen in the evening parked behind homes, and during the day crawling along dirt roads to employment, which nets each passenger about $6.50 for 12 hours of work.[19]

Carl and Audrey Brenner remember that the worst poverty they observed was in barrios of Texas and Oregon for migrant workers. The "homes" were like pigpens. There were rows of dilapidated shacks, kids on top of one another, and filth everywhere.[20]

Elly Saltzman considered an ironic contrast:

Our time in Mora [New Mexico] tested the fiber of each one in our group. The unique beauty of Mora Valley was unreal, juxtaposed to the harsh and stark poverty of its inhabitants. This county statistically ranks second under the heading of poverty. Welfare, food stamps, and illness are characteristic of this society. Without the assistance of the government, people would be destitute, economically and socially. And yet a gaze away is the beauty of the Sangre de Christo Mountains.[21]

One of Saltzman's campers experienced what many AJSS campers have discovered: the work is not always welcomed by those it is designed to benefit. Donna Arzt, who noted how odd it was to be called "Anglo" ("Funny thing to hear. I've been called an American. A Jew. Even a German. Never thought of myself that way before."), struggled to comprehend:

I'm beginning... trying... to understand the man we worked for today. He and his family stood on the sidelines but refused to work with us. Why? Was he proud of us, because he took pictures of our group?... It must have been a very difficult step for him to apply for help. Maybe he wasn't quite ready yet to take the next step, to work with us. For as hard as it is for us to understand him, it is that much harder for him to comprehend how "Anglos" could come to work for him... Going on welfare, asking for help, admitting you can't do it yourself, that's degrading for any man.[22]

As Jacqueline Jones has pointed out, the foreign migrant worker has no authority and few to champion him. Even if a naturalized citizen, he is so often on the move that he makes up no one's constituency. If an illegal immigrant, he doesn't dare to open his mouth. Though the huge numbers of ethnic Mexicans in farm work probably began as an historic accident (During World War II most American-born farmhands found themselves in the army or acquired much higher paying war economy jobs, so the federal government "temporarily" admitted *braceros* to replace them), growers now routinely rely on them to adjust to exploitative conditions not normally possible in representative democracy. After World War II, "Mexican immigration spilled out of the relatively narrow confines established under this program, as workers south of the Texas border responded to increased demand for farm laborers in all areas of the United States; in 1949 at least half a million illegal aliens were at work, most of them on the West Coast."[23]

The life that Jones details below has been confirmed by AJSS volunteers in several projects.

> Poor housing conditions were inextricably linked to poor health among migrants. Tin shacks and ramshackle barracks were cramped quarters for families, too hot to enter until after sundown on a blistering summer day. Leaky walls and roofs in drafty quarters and primitive sanitary facilities, combined with poor nutrition and arduous field work, took their toll in the form of respiratory and intestinal diseases. Predictably, the corollary of ill health was inadequate and, too often, inaccessible health care; as a result, migrants accepted readily identifiable forms of sickness as their "normal' condition." – like diarrhea in kids.[24]
>
> Migrant labor was even more exploitative than work in the manufacturing and service sectors, no matter how poorly paid. Throughout the twentieth century, migrants consistently received wages that amounted to from one-third to one-half the annual pay for unskilled factory jobs, but even these figures were generous, since up to 40 percent of their earnings consisted of non-monetary compensation in the form of transportation, food, and housing."[25]

I was an eyewitness to such devastating living conditions while directing two work projects in the mid-1990s. My introduction to Idaho and Texas came in areas overwhelmingly populated by ethnic Mexicans. In McAllen, Texas, AJSS was just eight miles from the Mexican border, but Idaho? The visitor's presumptions are jarred by the reality of postwar American agricultural life.

The Idaho Migrant Council hosted the 1996 project in Twin Falls, Idaho, part of the agricultural plains – really irrigated desert – that surround the Snake River as it curves through the southern portion of the state.

> The work of that organization [I wrote in the directors' report] is one of the great unknown success stories. In large part because of a remarkable advertising campaign, most Americans know no more about Idaho than potatoes. A picture of a solitary rancher hauling his spuds to market (probably on a horse) is the mistaken image that is created. To

be sure, Idaho produces potatoes – and wheat, hay, beet sugar, and mint, among other agricultural crops. But with a population of about one million, Idaho's agriculture is dependent on over 350,000 migrant and semi-migrant workers. These workers are overwhelmingly Hispanic, with the large majority Mexican in national origin. Still, because so many are migrants, they have failed to exercise political power in proportion to their numbers. For many years they were ignored, subject to ethnic prejudice and physical neglect. To address their needs the Idaho Migrant Council was founded. Today the Council is involved in a host of social and educational programs aimed at aiding these migrant workers.

Their housing division has provided hundreds of units of housing across the state. By far the largest housing development under their control was the site of the AJSS's efforts this summer in Twin Falls. Called *El Milagro* (the Miracle), this site containing over 100 units of housing was built originally as a detention center for Japanese Americans during World War II. That shameful chapter was continued when the shacks were taken over by the Idaho Growers Association after the war. Providing no services – no roads, no sewers – the growers literally allowed the houses to rot before asking the Migrant Council to buy what was called "the work camp." While no one wants to operate a slum, the Migrant Council was unwilling to abandon the hundreds of individuals who would otherwise go homeless. Developing a 12 point plan, Migrant Council leaders undertook the transformation of the project into *El Milagro*, putting in roads, a sewer system, transforming barracks into attractive two and three bedroom apartments, and beginning the construction of a community center.[26]

The Idaho Migrant Council is the perfect illustration of the successes and failures of the War on Poverty. Precisely the kind of local organization OEO officials would fund, the Migrant Council had great ambitions. With over a third of a million migrants in desperate need of improved housing, education, health services, and citizenship orientation, the Migrant Council – whose leaders are entirely Mexican-Americans – could lend their constituents a sense of empowerment and belonging. But the Johnson Administration's commitment to this war was miniscule compared to the colossal war it fought and lost abroad. Furthermore, with its failure to bring immediate results, and with several community organizations voicing political opinions distasteful to many politicians, the anti-poverty programs received ever fewer funds, until the Reagan reaction reduced the flow to a dripping trickle. The Idaho Migrant Council was justly proud of producing hundreds of housing units, but there were hundreds of thousands of migrants needing adequate shelter.

El Milagro was a miracle by comparison to what it had been, but to AJSS volunteers it bore little resemblance to adequate housing. 47 small two bedroom shacks looked like neglected bungalows in a resort with no recreation facilities. Migrant Council efforts had already installed indoor plumbing and tiny but functioning kitchens; sewers had been sunk beneath newly paved roads. Still, five male Jewish teenagers crowded into one of these units. Their bodies and their suitcases filled the cottage. It was difficult for the AJSS volunteers to imagine whole families living inside these permanently as some – the most fortunate tenants – did. Those who had managed to secure a job beyond the seasonal harvesting of crops, perhaps by working in the sugar beet processing plants nearby, lived in *El Milagro* through the winter. More than half of the cottages were inhabited by long-term residents.

These older cottages surrounded two-unit buildings which were renovated sheds. Each unit was arranged as a railroad flat with a kitchen and two bedrooms. Recently sided and given new sheetrock walls, these units were new but surprisingly small. The nine girls on the project took up all of the floor space in one; again it was difficult to imagine a family fitting furniture inside the rooms.

The Migrant Council had erected a community center with a large meeting room in an effort to create the feeling of neighborhood. During the summer of 1996, it was still unfinished, though AJSS labor was only used to build offices during the final week of the stay. As yet surrounded by unseeded dirt, the center was then an austere place; when it rained the muddy imprint of work boots soiled the new linoleum.

The main project was the long overdue painting of the 47 single unit cottages. Daily, campers scraped, primed and painted the exterior of all of the buildings. It was a strange experience. Assured by the work supervisor, *El Milagro* resident director Rudy Rodriguez, that the residents knew their houses were to be painted, campers nonetheless felt awkward about painting the homes of those with people inside. Most of the residents left before dawn and came home after dusk – in Idaho in July this is before 5 A.M. and after 10 P.M. - ample testimony to the difficulty of their labor, but some children, the elderly, and mothers of large families remained home.

Campers longed to have contact with the neighbors whose houses they painted; a few of the local children occasionally "hung out" and chatted with the volunteers. Alicia Nathan remembered her experience with them:

ALL FOR THE CHILDREN
They awaited our arrival each morning
the grins on their faces
brothers, sisters, cousins
the audience to our paint job
many parents seemed far from enthused
at times we felt like intruders
however the children did welcome us
sitting by the windows scraping
the paint coming off slowly
we were exposed to the conversations

> along with the unique way of life in *El Milagro*
> we heard stories of abuse
> stories of abused lives
> not only did we hear
> but experienced first hand
> and witnessed
> Aaron and Candy not play kickball
> it was the fifteenth of the month, Daddy got paid
> a family excursion to McDonald's was the regular
> every two weeks
> Casey and Christopher are sent to scavenge
> that is food they can not afford
> Robert was too busy to play
> he had to fish for dinner
> I ask myself why am I painting houses
> rather than putting effort into the children
> trying to better the lives of these less fortunate
> actually we are here to better the lives
> we, AJSS, are improving the conditions
> we have painted forty-seven houses in *El Milagro*
> painting the houses we peeled off the old
> we refurbished the homes the task was not easy
> the unappreciative adults brought my spirits down
> once a "hello" was not returned
> nor a nod or a grin
> no acknowledgment killed my enthusiasm
> I wondered the reason to continue
> why should I apply all I have
> to help these people, although needy
> who seem to treat me as an intruder
> I then realized my importance
> if not for the adults, then
> all for the children.[27]

Less eloquently, the whole group noticed the lack of response from the adult residents. Simone Isturis, with the advantage of Spanish language fluency, nonetheless "realized how it was to feel like an outsider: everyone was different from me. I felt like they looked at me and laughed. I finally understood how it was to be different."[28]

Much more troubling was the tension surrounding the camp. One evening several of the girls awoke to discover a young man in their room; he smelled of beer. The following day Rudy Rodriguez assured the group the intruder had simply wandered into the wrong room. But a young unwed mother who was the focus of a great deal of male interest occupied the other unit in the girls' building. Jacqueline Jones has commented that the terrible anxiety of migrant camp life gives rise to a culture of "swaggering bravado" of "brandishing knives and picking fights."[29] After two weeks in *El Milagro* the AJSS girls witnessed an explosion of this culture in front of their window. A quarrel over their next door neighbor's attention led to young men stabbing and rock throwing; one of the volunteers was scratched by a fragment of glass. The sudden flash of violence was terrifying education; the next day the group moved into the dorms of a local community college and commuted to *El Milagro* for the rest of the summer. For the following week, campers warily watched cars to see if they matched those of the young men involved in the fight. Although they continued to feel proud of the work they accomplished, it was impossible to build a sense of camaraderie with anyone save Rudy and the office staff.

A less dangerous sense of "otherness" was produced when Rudy directed the volunteers to a rodeo in a town an hour away. The annual event celebrating Independence Day was in the town of Rupert; hundreds crammed the stadium and enjoyed the carnival booths outside. The group had a fine time, but it seemed strange that virtually everyone was Latino. Spanish was the most frequently heard tongue. Along the Snake River agricultural belt, this is typical of Idaho, contrasting vividly with Boise to the east and the Shoshone Mountains national forest area to the north. It is also the composition of most of the farm country producing America's abundant produce.

AJSS interaction with ethnic Mexicans has been greatest in Texas; six projects between 1970 and 1997 have linked the New York based organization to a variety of associations aimed at producing a better life for the Chicano population. In 1970 the sponsor was the most publicly known advocate for migrant workers, then at the height of popular acclaim, the United Farm Workers. At a time when trade unions had lost public favor and when organizing had all but dried up, the UFW's campaign among pickers in California, particularly in the grape fields, galvanized popular support. A nation-wide boycott of grapes succeeded in organizing significant numbers of agricultural workers. Given the catastrophes the labor movement had experienced in previous attempts, even during the great expansion of unionism in the 1930s, the UFW's success was attributable to the hard work of its organizers, the charisma of leader Cesar Chavez, and a successful publicity campaign exposing the impoverishment of migrant life.

Organizing among South Texas farm hands, the UFW sought the construction of a building which would operate as an all-purpose service center for the migrants. The AJSS contingent was scheduled to work on the center, but bureaucratic and funding delays involved the organization instead in demolition, clerical work, painting and day care center responsibility. The latter activity exposed the volunteers to the poverty of individual children; the fiasco with funding made clear how strapped were even those organizations which would try to help. The Brenners reported that "Because the people had no materials, nor the money to purchase materials, it appeared they could not be helped. A local campaign was initiated by us for materials and the response was astonishing." Once materials were collected, volunteers began painting and repairing inside homes, so that "for the first time the campers became aware of the poverty that exists among the migrant farm workers."[30]

The UFW won at least one convert among the volunteers. Camper David Giber wrote:

> Here in the valley, the human feeling of a great people resurging into new self-awareness is a feeling that gradually takes hold of you, until it fills you with an overwhelming excitement and, for me, a distant sense of participating in something wonderfully and deeply human. You look at the sky, at the faces around you, and suddenly you are no longer building a floor where yesterday children slept on dirt; you are in a massive crowd of people – yelling, chanting, crying. And the cries, be they in Spanish or English, are for one thing: human dignity.
>
> For those of us from New York whose relatives were liberated from the oppressive sweatshops and the rotting tenements, we know the vehicle of change; it is unionization. The union system has overcome many of the faults inherent in our economic system, and has brought most American workers to a living standard of comfort and dignity . . .
>
> Although I have gone through many weeks here, I know I have hardly gotten my feet wet. But it's better to take a step into the turbulent sea of revolution (though you may not know specifically where you are going) than to remain on the dry land of comfort and respectability, priding yourself on the "liberal progress" you've made. Those on the dry land will soon be washed away and drowned; those already swimming will make it to shore.[31]

Thirteen years later, Jules and Julianne Hirsh led a contingent to the same area, working with the Hidalgo County Economic Development Agency to weatherize and improve the homes of the poor, almost all of them Chicano. Housed in McAllen, the Hirshes found little welcome from the Jewish community, which remembered and resented the Brenners' earlier visit. Several of the synagogue members were growers and were hostile to the UFW.[32]

In 1997, the AJSS again returned to McAllen, this time hosted by Rio Grande Habitat for Humanity. Much of the grim picture had changed, but much more remained to be accomplished.

The work itself was the best indication that positive steps were being undertaken. The nineties' boom was being extended to some of those normally forgotten.

McAllen was riding a wave of prosperity as a sister city to the *maquilladora* center in Reynosa, Mexico. American factories south of the border employed Mexican workers to assemble products for distribution in the United States; McAllen enjoyed an expansion of shipping and warehousing jobs. A vastly expanding hospital system that appealed to the Mexican middle class was creating thousands of new jobs. McAllen's always mild weather gave it a 12 month growing season and made it a center for tourism in the winter. The prosperity created induced the city to help fund the creation of a vast working class neighborhood called *Los Encinos*. 300 three-bedroom homes were being constructed surrounding a newly built modern school, complete with elaborate park and athletic fields. The homes looked like vintage middle class housing, though the rooms were not large; inexpensive brick from Mexico gave the buildings a prosperous look. The city installed electricity, sewer, and plumbing lines at no cost to the homeowners and initiated public bus service to downtown McAllen. The tax assessment of the new residences was kept well below market levels. Ten of the 300 homes were assigned to Rio Grande Habitat, which made them available to families with incomes between $12,000 and $25,000.

The AJSS group squeezed into one of the three-bedroom homes while working on three others. Next door was a Habitat family. The father's income from his job as a Pep Boy mechanic qualified him for a home. The family of five thus moved into a stable working class community with a great chance to escape the horrors of the *colonias*, the "housing" so many Mexican and Mexican Americans living in Texas had endured for 50 years.

Campers were introduced to the old alternative through the efforts of Temple Emmanuel Rabbi David Lipper, and his uncle, businessman Michael J. Blum. Lipper and Blum gave continued thoughtful attention to the contingent while it was in McAllen. Nothing was more valuable than the education they provided. After the directors arranged a bus, Blum guided the group over the border to Reynosa and into a *maquilladora* factory. Skeptical campers grilled factory manager Darrell Price. Though the factory was clean, the group noticed that the work force entirely consisted of people in their twenties or younger. Price confirmed that all the factories in Reynosa paid a uniform wage and benefit package; campers concluded that this would not be sufficient to maintain families, so after a few years workers had to move on.

More illuminating still, the bus passed through some of the old McAllen *colonias* on the way back. Here AJSS volunteers got to see the normal way of life for Mexican and Mexican-American farm workers who did not get into *Los Encinos*. Dirt roads carried the bus past homes with no sewers or electricity and in desperate need of repair.

Two additional trips to Mexico taught the group more than it wanted to know about poverty. In Monterrey, a city of over one million, the AJSS vans drove past tens of thousands of cardboard and corrugated metal shacks. The public buses were of every conceivable model; the only visible connection was that every one looked ready for the scrap heap. All had broken windows and rusty panels, and most sent up billows of black smoke. The filth along the main streets made the worst slums of New York City look pristine. Downtown were impressive public buildings and heroic sculptures; virtually no one was out to observe these attractions. Towards the end of the summer, the contingent visited the border town of Progresso, parking on the American side and walking over the Rio Grande by footbridge to avoid stopping at customs. Progresso is a town made for American tourists; it is a long block of artifact shops. The main currency is the American dollar and the dominant feeling is the ugliness of poverty. Walking across the footbridge, tourists are surrounded on both sides by young boys standing in the puddle which is the Rio Grande on the Gulf side; they lift six to eight foot poles which hold cups. Like everyone in Progresso, what they want is American money.

The people on the streets are tiny; the adults are mostly shorter than five feet tall; the children are correspondingly small for their ages. One wonders if this is genetics or malnutrition. It is impossible to walk any three-foot stretch without being besieged by beggars. How Americans enjoy their time in such a place is a mystery.

One sign of the times is in what the 1997 project did not do. The Brenners in 1970 and the Hirshes in 1983 took their groups to Mexico City; by 1997 the reputation of the capital – burgeoning with newly displaced people, illness, crime, and pollution – made such a trip seem foolhardy and dangerous.

Even recreation trips northward provided an education in ugliness. Twice the group headed to San Antonio; twice one glance into the vans by guards 100 miles from the border resulted in quick invitations to move on. But cars containing people with darker skins were routinely searched exhaustively. Was this drug vigilance or plain old racism? Each camper had his or her own theory.

The exposure to racism and graphic impoverishment made the work seem more valuable. American poverty comes in many guises. When seen at its worst, it lends urgency to the work being accomplished. Camper Jesse Halpern wrote, "The homes that we build will allow a family to have something of their own they can be proud of. When we asked that little girl Samantha if she was getting her own room, her smile brightened up the day. Getting a smile from a little girl is what the world should be about." AJSS labor enabled three brick homes to rise in six weeks. Three more families could be saved from the *colonias*.[34]

The federal government's abandonment of the War in Poverty returned local organizing to the auspices of the religious institutions which had carried the ball before Lyndon Johnson had convinced congress that the elimination of want was the job of national politicians. Traditional charitable groups like the Salvation Army, The Society of St. Vincent de Paul and Catholic Charities were among those attempting to fill this need. Although successful in many localities, these institutions might be limited because they already sprang from narrow constituencies like individual church sects. What was needed was a new organization with resources, a broad constituency, and no clear allegiances to known sectarian interests. In the 1970s, that organization took shape in a religious cooperative in Georgia and in the desperate need of Zaire.

Millard and Linda Fuller, wealthy millionaires living a life of materialisitc abundance and emotional deprivation, turned to a Christian farming cooperative in Georgia for spiritual help. Koinonia had survived since 1942 despite its opposition to racism and its gently radical tilt on many social questions. Fuller's discussion with Koinonia's leaders led to proposals for a fund to be established by wealthy contributors as the basis for developing housing. The donations would be used as seed money to be borrowed – not given away – and meant to encourage those in need to work with volunteers. Since labor would be free overall costs would remain low so that people who could not have considered owning their own homes would have the potential to do so.

The Fullers tested their concept in Zaire, seeking to create housing for 2,000. After getting the new program underway, they returned to the United States to establish Habitat for Humanity International in 1976. Former President Jimmy Carter's adoption of Habitat as a central component of his life in 1984 won the organization public attention and greatly facilitated its growth.[35]

Though each local Habitat has considerable autonomy, its basic features include the following: Each Habitat family must put in a set number of hours of sweat equity to qualify for a home. While some work is contracted out (This varies from one locality to another; some Habitats contract for roofing; some contract for electricity), depending on local building codes and which professionals are providing free or nearly free services, most of the work is handled by the families and volunteer groups. When materials are donated, they are of course accepted; contractors feel a social obligation to keep material costs down. Habitat locals with influence pressure city or county governments to cede them land or to sell building lots at low costs. The total cost to Habitat is the total mortgage for the homeowner; it is held at no interest for a 30-year term. Income requirements are between the minimum that can conceivably support the monthly mortgage fee – Habitat families must have steady jobs – and a maximum low enough to prevent the homeowner from buying a residence in a traditional manner. These numbers vary from one community to another; we have seen that in McAllen in 1997 the range was between $12,000 and $25,000.

To broaden support, an organizer of a local Habitat carefully invites all the religious organizations of a community to join the Habitat board. Though self-consciously Christian (in a theology not all that different from the prophetic Judaism of Ferdinand Isserman), local Jewish and Muslim temples are invited to participate as well. One of the elements that has made Habitat successful is that it has succeeded in drawing the support of several churches wherever it functions. Thus it is not associated with a particular church, but with the more generalized notion that helping one's neighbor is the job of all of God's people. With many or most of a locality's religious institutions represented, local politicians, businesses, and community organizations are more easily persuaded to cooperate.

Another element that enabled Habitat to thrive even as it grew during the Reagan era was contained in the slogan, "A hand up, not a hand out." Since the recipients of the housing had to labor for their homes, and since they were to be ultimately responsible to handle the costs, Habitat houses were seen as encouraging its families to live stable, viable lives.

The success of the idea has been breathtaking. As the organization notes, "Habitat for Humanity International has built and rehabilitated some 80,000 houses with families in need, becoming a true world leader in addressing the issues of poverty housing."[36]

Between 1986 and 1999 AJSS groups were hosted by local Habitats nine times. Though conditions vary from one locality to the next, Habitat is often an excellent patron. Its extensive resources in the community make it easier for the sponsor to provide housing and transportation resources; most important for the success of the program, there is planned and ongoing work for the summer volunteers to connect with.

Another element that makes for a meaningful summer is the interaction between families doing their sweat equity and the AJSS volunteers. Selma's McDonald's provided a chance meeting between the Murray family, recipient of one of two homes AJSS campers built in 1993, and several of the volunteers. One of the Murray children, an eight-year-old girl, was pouting. When she was introduced to "the boys and girls who are building our house," she broke into a deep smile that brightened the week for the Jewish teenagers. Similar interactions between Habitat families and the volunteers made work meaningful in all of the localities.

More lasting still is the quality interaction when the sweat equity becomes full time work with Habitat. In Selma, Steve Travis, already living in a Habitat home, was hired as a second work supervisor during the AJSS stay. Charismatic Steve became an icon to the teenagers working with him. His unfailing good humor, technical competence, and unstinting generosity made him an inspiration for work. On the last day, campers worked overtime with him to try to finish the sheetrocking of the Millhouse home.

Mike Monroe's direction of the building of his own straw bale house in Wyoming was the pathway to understanding of the values of the Arapaho and of the model self-direction of a Habitat family.

In 1999, Habitat sponsored all three AJSS projects. Jonathan Hirsh and Karin Kaiser brought a contingent to work and sweat in Albany, Georgia. This is home territory for the organization; scores of homes had already been erected. Here the AJSS felt the downside of Habitat's success. Used to having volunteer adult church groups working at top speed for a week, the local supervisor insisted on an 8 – 5:30 day, with no allowances for the heat. It took some mediation to make allowances for the longer commitment of the teenagers from the east before both sides were satisfied. Naturally, the group toured the international headquarters in

Americus, Georgia; they came away awed by the models of housing from around the world and the sheer size of the operation: 500 employees labor in the international's home office.[37]

Henry Kohn has found, in calling some Habitat operations, that several refuse to budge to accommodate the needs of a large group staying for several weeks. Many localities now are teeming with ardent church groups whose congregations collect funds to donate to the local sponsor and who provide their own work supervision and transportation. These groups tend to be smaller and can afford to pay for local housing. In these localities, some Habitat organizations are not eager to accommodate AJSS needs.

In addition Kohn resists making his organization an "appendage" of the newer one. AJSS has worked with scores of sponsors; the variety of work that has developed has enriched the experience of the volunteers.

Still, Habitat work has often been meaningful. In 1999, the fledgling Habitat of Marquette Michigan built four homes. AJSS labor contributed to all four, though the last was just getting underway as the summer ended. Again the most meaningful relationship developed between the teenagers and Gary Nurenberg, a Habitat homeowner whose sweat equity turned into full time work supervision. Nurenberg had been bed-ridden until May, semi-paralyzed after back surgery. He and his wife Barbara cared for three children and were still grieving for the young child lost to chronic illness. Knowing he had to work to earn his house, Gary forced himself out of bed. He was on his feet less than two months when AJSS volunteers met him on the work site. There he became their coworker and friend, directing them in each phase of the work while awing the campers with his physical strength and courage. During the last two weeks, AJSS volunteers worked with Gary on his own house, making every nail driven a testimony to friendship.

Working side-by-side with Steve Travis, Mike Monroe, and Gary Nurenberg, AJSS campers have seen one face of the poor in America, recognizing the best that humanity has to offer.

6

Changing Judaism, Changing America

Concerned at mid-century with the erosion of Jewish identity, Rabbis Hoffman, Isserman, and Lelyveld could hardly have anticipated the impact of prosperity and suburbanization on American Jewry. The unforeseen post-war prosperity experienced by the majority of Americans created a seemingly universal desire for automobile, home, and television set. Middle and working class families could afford the mobility of the car; this in turn made new, less expensive housing outside the city limits practical. The magic of the entertainment box inside the home made it possible for families to dispense with the richer and more varied culture available in the city center.

In the early days of the American Jewish Society for Service, the developing movement of Jews out of New York City towards the surrounding suburbs or the parallel movement of Jews to the south and west had little effect. By the middle 1950s and throughout most of the next ten years, the majority of participants were New York City residents. Many came from older Jewish conclaves in Manhattan on the upper west or upper east side, traditional Jewish neighborhoods (which had been the original Jewish suburbs[1]) like Flatbush in Brooklyn, and the early post-war "suburbs" within the city like Jamaica Estates or Little Neck in Queens. Prosperous communities just outside the city limits like Great Neck on Long Island or Scarsdale in Westchester soon began providing a substantial share of AJSS campers.[2]

The world of New York Jewry is unique. From the 1920s through at least the 1970s, Jews were the largest single ethnic group in America's most populous city. The two to three million Jews living in the nation's greatest city were more than the total number of people living in any other metropolis in the nation, other than Los Angeles and Chicago. Jewish neighborhoods consisting of tens of thousands or hundreds of thousands of people provided a feeling of such protected insularity that individual Christians seemed like aberrations.

As many writers have noted, growing up in such communities provided a sense of Jewish identity without residents needing to act. Immigrant elders conversing with one another in Yiddish, the presence of Yiddish language

93

newspapers on the newsstands, and kosher butcher shops, bakeries selling rye bread and delicatessens closed on Saturdays but open Sundays all told Jewish youngsters who they were even if they never set foot in a temple.[3] In New York, many Jews rarely did. Marshall Sklare explains, "It is clear that in the larger communities, and especially in New York, synagogue membership does not have high symbolic significance. Accordingly, since many people lack the feeling that Jewish identity requires synagogue membership, non-affiliation does not mean a vote for assimilation."[4]

The New York City millions, descended in large numbers from the massive eastern European emigration of 1880-1920, were often entirely secular in their composition. As Charles S. Liebman writes, "The important fact to be noted is that a disproportionately large number of them [the immigrants], relative to a cross-section of East European Jewry, were nontraditionalists, secularist Jews, Socialists and Zionists. A few of them, particularly the Socialists, were militantly anti-religious." Those who weren't political had a "folk" religion of heritage without piety.[5] Being Jewish meant identifying with a cultural tradition of social justice. While one could draw a line from the moral authority of the biblical prophets to the militant dissent of these immigrants, many of the most active Jewish trade unionists or socialists could not have, so divorced was their own activity from the world of the synagogue.

Many of the children and grandchildren of these secular, political immigrant Jews were participants in early AJSS projects in the 1950s and 1960s. It is little wonder that several projects in the early days featured contentious arguments about kosher-style eating, that rabbi project directors had some difficulty in communicating with their charges, and that Elly Saltzman and, briefly, Ed Cohen were cast as members of the establishment by volunteers who demanded the open defiance of Jim Crow legislation. Idealistic teenagers who wished to participate in service often sprang from politically conscious, if not necessarily observant, Jewish families. Some of the impassioned rhetoric of David Giber after his 1970 experience in McAllen, Texas must be rooted in a family perspective older than himself.

By 1970, of course, adolescents had more than their grandparents' ethos to create a political and social conscience. The rousing battles of the civil rights movement stirred AJSS campers before their summer experiences. When Rabbi Lelyveld was beaten in Mississippi during the 1964 voter registration campaign, AJSS project directors informed their charges of the activities of one of their founders; campers wrote letters of support and Lelyveld thanked them for their concern.[6]

The development of the peace movement further galvanized political consciousness. As we have seen, the anti-war politics of the Ripley, Tennessee group contributed to the tension between the volunteers and an already hostile white community.

On a more practical level, late 1960s social values caused a different kind of trouble. The Brenners found dealing with smuggled marijuana to be a recurrent motif during their early days as project directors.[7] While such conflicts caused anxiety for the responsible adults, conversations with the teenagers about respecting the cultural mores of those being serviced were among their more valuable learning experiences.

Despite the increased level of political and social rebelliousness among the campers of the anti-war generation, the overall trend among AJSS applicants, as among the Jewish population as a whole, has been one of increasing compatibility with the larger suburban trend which has engulfed the United States. Though New York City campers continue to be represented on virtually every project, in recent summers there have often been only one or two from the five boroughs. The New York metropolitan area still fills the majority of the project rosters, but campers are more likely to live in northern New Jersey, Westchester county, or on eastern Long Island than they are to live in the city itself. As the decades have passed, the volunteers tend to be less politically sophisticated and committed, although they are equally enthusiastic about service as a positive way of asserting their Jewish identity.

Most sociologists and historians of modern American Judaism have noticed an apparent paradox. As Jews have left the metropolitan area, the mushrooming of synagogue buildings, the growth in the absolute numbers of congregation membership and the rise in the percentage of synagogue members among the Jewish population all indicate increased self-identification as Jews and greater involvement with the faith's sacramental customs. But virtually all studies bewail the contradiction between synagogue membership and commitment to traditional Jewish practice. Most have confirmed the findings most famously described in Marshall Sklare's study of a midwestern Jewish suburb during the 1960s. In Lakeville (a fictitious name) Sklare surveyed the residents on eleven sacramental practices covering Jewish dietary laws, Sabbath observances, and the honoring of Jewish holidays. He found a majority of his survey group practiced two customs only: lighting candles on Hanukkah and conducting a seder on Passover. He speculated that these were annual observances and therefore easier to fulfill, but so was fasting on Yom Kippur, which did not command great support. He further noted that observing Hanukkah, the most popular of the eleven practices, allowed Jews to approximate the American observance of Christmas.[8]

Nor were Sklare's group more likely to prove truly observant. While almost every one of the surveyed was a current or past member of a synagogue, only 13% of them attended regularly, down 24% from their parents. Most attended only on the High Holy Days.[9] Arthur Hertzberg compared Jewish religious practice to those of their neighbors: "Atheism is no longer a recognizable force in the American Jewish community, though it was quite prevalent in the immigrant radical movements fifty years ago." Jews belong to congregations in percentages equal to Christians, "but it is notorious that, except for the High Holidays, synagogue attendance is radically lower than church attendance... half of the enrolled Christians... go to church regularly on Sunday; no more than one, or at most two, in ten of Jews who belong to a synagogue are there regularly at the Sabbath services." Again, many more among Jewish college students as opposed to their gentile classmates called themselves atheists, and few went to High Holy Day services while on or near a campus.[10]

If Jews did not truly find their religion compelling, why did they build and join synagogues with what might be called religious fervor as they journeyed from city to suburb or from the northeast to the sunbelt? Most social scientists believe that lacking an environment including the Yiddish tongue, Yiddish newspapers, Yiddish theater, Jewish shopping areas and a unique political culture, the children of Yiddishkeit, now adults, found synagogue membership and financial aid to Israel (supplemented by an eventual summer vacation there) as the viable ways to express a Jewish identity. In many new suburbs, choosing between a Reform and a Conservative synagogue was less a theological decision than one governed by social networks and convenience. In practical terms, the services available at the Jewish Community Center were often far more compelling to the membership than those of the temple; even though the only element obviously Jewish about the J.C.C. might be its name. Jack Wertheimer writes:

> [While] the young families moving to suburbia in the 1940s and early 1950s often had only scant exposure to synagogue life prior to the move... After moving to suburbia, transplanted urbanites found themselves lonely for Jewish companionship. They discovered a need for a synagogue to anchor them on the suburban frontier and provide a network of Jewish friends and peers... the synagogue was a surrogate for the Jewish neighborhood... In the absence of a Jewish neighborhood where youngsters were socialized in Jewish customs and behaviors through an unconscious osmotic process, it became necessary for parents to affiliate with a synagogue that would serve as a surrogate agent for education.[11]

Thus it is not surprising that the typical volunteer on an AJSS service project often arrives with a hazy understanding of what his or her Judaism is. A typical cross-section of the campers includes two or three active members of the Conservative and Reform Jewish youth groups (United Synagogue Youth and National Conference of Synagogue Youth), two or three students of Jewish day schools, and five or more whose families rarely, if ever, attend synagogue. Some of the latter are children of mixed marriages, hardly a wonder, for the percentages of Jews marrying people of other faiths has grown exponentially with each decade of the post-war period, jumping to one in three by 1970. More recently, according to demographer Sidney Goldstein in 1990, "For every new couple consisting of two Jewish partners, there were approximately two new couples in which only one of the partners was Jewish."[12] From the earliest days, projects have also included a handful of gentile volunteers eager to give service and willing to accept the Jewish component as a condition of their participation. AJSS projects do not have Orthodox campers because while kosher-style meals are served, projects cannot often find kosher meat and because the weekend travel program would be seen by the Orthodox as a violation of Sabbath sacraments.

Informal interviews with campers who are members of USY and NCSY reveal a hunger among these adolescents for a fully developed cultural identity. Unfulfilled by the dominant consumer culture of their age, they seek to define themselves as Jews in order to lend meaning to their social activities. High school denotes them academically and chronologically, but it does not offer a consistent way for these individuals to describe themselves in the larger society. By engaging in peer created sacraments and secular events, these young people can add "Jewish" to the characteristics that delineate them as teenagers.

Those who come out of the Jewish day schools have less concern about the identity question than their parents. Often the children of people who removed themselves from cohesive inner-city Jewish neighborhoods, many AJSS volunteers attending day schools report that their parents, having moved to suburbs whose feel and look is identical to the gentile neighborhoods next door, seek to reify the identity of their children by enrolling them in separate educational institutions. Their logic is consistent with Conservative movement founder Solomon Schecter, who found in dominant Reform practice such a readiness to accommodate gentile culture that American Judaism itself was likely to evaporate. It is no accident that many of these schools bear Schecter's name.

But a curious contradiction has developed. While AJSS campers who come out of the day schools are far more aware of traditional practices than those who go to public school, they tend to be more questioning and sometimes more hostile to the sacramental activities that their friends don't even know about. In several of the projects directed by Catherine Kaczmarek Milkman and myself, day school campers have expressed hostility not to the increased rigor or length of their school day – about which they have acceptance and pride – but to what they perceive as the rigidity of their religious instruction and the received faith's defiance of intellectual logic. More expressions of agnosticism and atheism have been heard from these day school participants than from their colleagues, who tend to be indifferent about religious tenets.[13]

Jewish day school students at AJSS projects have lent the Friday night services fuller structure and provided all participants with a greater understanding of Jewish ritual practices.

The importance of the AJSS experience for a small sampling of both urban and suburban youngsters has been central in defining their Judaism. Sklare sees the issue as an individual one:

> The discussion of Jewish identity may, in fact, constitute for the modern Jew a kind of pious act of the type which he is not capable of performing in respect to certain more traditional manifestations of his identity. From this perspective talking about Jewish identity is an act of affirmation, and Jewishness remains alive as long as the individual is troubled by the problem of identity.[14]

The AJSS group setting and the constant discussions of service as a lifelong commitment to the prophetic ideal have proven to be precisely the "act of affirmation" Hoffman, Isserman, and Lelyveld hoped it would be when they envisioned a Jewish service organization, not for most, but for a thoughtful subgroup of AJSS campers. As a positive way of defining Judaism for the young people who participate, it may well be a central experience. Ed Cohen remembers that Stanley Herr, now on the AJSS board and a prominent attorney and scholar, as a camper wanted nothing to do with religion. One evening Cohen was with the religion committee singing melodies for the upcoming service and young Herr was "captivated by the melody." He sat down and listened and then told Cohen, "If you need somebody to chant, I'd be interested."[15]

A month after his service project ended, Herr wrote to Henry Kohn to explain how his 1963 experience working in Cherokee, North Carolina awakened his dormant Judaism:

> At the outset of the summer I must admit that I was quite skeptical of the religious program. I am not an observant Jew, although I feel a strong cultural identity with our people. Several weeks of casual observance seemed like a sham for one who had neglected his religious heritage and whose ignorance of its practices and beliefs I most shamefully admit is abysmal.
>
> It was thus that in one evening's pre-dinner reading late in the summer I was struck by the line, "you are Israel." Now the notion of Jewish survival is not new to me and is something that I am in total agreement with, but previously I had felt that there would be many to insure its continuance. But what if, as my own contacts with fellow Jews had shown me, nearly everyone is as unsure and unconfirmed in his religion as I? Without an articulate group of first-class minds to sustain Judaism, through the dilution of faith and of identity which occurs with the passage of each succeeding generation, our religion would be fated to oblivion. And what a tragedy this would be if our civilization survived through several millennia of ruthless persecutions and pressures, only to be extinguished in an age of tolerance and liberality.
>
> I realize that what I am saying is not a new discovery, only my responsibilities are. Since returning home I have set out to correct my lack of knowledge by a thorough reading program, and I am

> reexamining a matter which I had previously shut the door on as a closed matter. It is not a religious fervor that moves me, just the desire to review something which I feel that my first cursory view may have looked over.[16]

Other campers have expressed awareness of a self-conscious Jewish awakening while toiling on AJSS work projects.

Occasionally the work itself has taken on a religious quality. A recent project in Wisconsin provided an AJSS contingent with the opportunity to work with their hands to mend the human spirit.

> What is a more poignant sign of the current urban scene than the construction of a park dedicated to the 214 Milwaukee children who have died between 1987 and 1997 in acts of random violence? Called the *Victory over Violence Park* on Martin Luther King Drive, it memorializes these innocent victims with two huge V's in tan concrete artistically erected at a 45 degree angle in what had formerly been a vacant lot of weeds. Our campers cleared the area, built brick sidewalks and a wall, installed trees and shrubs. Parents of the dead told our campers how much this beautiful park means to them as a tribute to the loved ones they lost. The purpose of the park is to focus on the scourge of violence and to create a dialogue and momentum to stem the tide of violence.[17]

Experiences like these, prominently featured in the AJSS newsletter, which began at four pages and was instituted as an annual report in December 1960 (it is now a fully illustrated 12 page brochure), became the basis for recruiting. In its second decade, the organization expanded its outreach. By 1961 it was possible to field two summer projects; the following summer there were three, though only six campers accompanied the Saltzmans to Israel. That experiment proved frustrating to the project directors, who were asked to cede authority over the group to the project hosts, the Israel Guide Dog Foundation for the Blind.[18] It marked the only time an AJSS project has been assigned outside the continental United States, and this is unlikely to occur again. But the decade continued to push the organization's outreach further southward and westward, through the plains states and into Montana and Arizona.[19] Stanley Herr was one of 50 AJSS campers at three Indian reservations in 1963.

Riding high on the idealism unleashed by a decade of student activism and the demographics of the baby boom, the organization was able to briefly expand to four projects in the early 1970s. Since then most summers have seen three AJSS contingents scattered throughout the nation, although the society went through lean times of skeletal two project summers during the late 1970s and early 1980s.[20]

After the sudden death of Hy Sankel, Henry Kohn's recruitment of Elly and Ruth Saltzman as project directors in 1959 began a linear continuity of site leadership. The Saltzmans served as project directors through 1973. Elly recruited Ed Cohen, his teaching colleague in Long Beach in 1961,[21] and he pursued Jules Hirsh, a fellow member of the Chautauqua Symphony Orchestra, for service beginning in 1962.[22] Hirsh mentioned the organization to Carl Brenner, but it was a Manhattan principal and friend of Henry Kohn's who urgently approached Brenner after Ed Cohen's heart attack forced him to retire from AJSS activity in June 1968. Although committed to a Catskill summer camp, the Brenners eagerly accepted the emergency assignment and directed for the next eleven summers.[23] After 26 summers the Hirshes have retired from the field, but their contacts carry on their tradition. Marty Kopelowitz was a new teacher at Midwood High School when Jules asked him to consider the AJSS. The Kopelowitzes have been project directors since 1972; in their final summer as directors in 2000 they surpassed the Hirshes in total number of projects supervised. Jules and Julianne's son Jonathan and his wife Karin Kaiser have been directing projects since 1989. The Midwood High School connection was mined again when Jules Hirsh approached his colleagues Paul and Catherine Kaczmarek Milkman, who began their AJSS experience in Selma, Alabama in 1993. While others have served for one or two summers, the couples mentioned have developed a passionate loyalty to the organization. For the Brenners, Kopelowitzes and the Hirshes, the AJSS experience is at the core of their Jewish identity.[24] At Henry Kohn's invitation, the Hirshes and the Brenners became members of the AJSS Board of Directors when they retired from the field; today Jules Hirsh is the organization's treasurer, Julianne Hirsh a committed organizer of special events, and the Brenners serve jointly as Executive Directors. In one summer newsletter Julianne Hirsh considered the meaning of the AJSS experience for herself:

> A dear friend of mine wrote to me at the beginning of the summer: "I hope your Crookston summer is adding another year's notch to your other summer experiences. You're both so matter-of-fact about it, but it really is such a great thing you're doing – I'm sure you must forget it, but perhaps you'd love yourselves more and even each other if you'd see yourselves as we see you. I pray for your strength."
>
> I pondered those thoughts a long time before I could answer her. This friend has a six year old little girl, an Apache Indian adopted at the age of three months. I've heard people say, "What a marvelous thing you're doing and isn't your daughter lucky to have you." And my friend has turned to me and said, "What crap! We adopted her because we wanted to and not for any glory in the eyes of others." So I wrote to her and said, "It's a little like your wanting to adopt an Indian child. I do it because I want to. I enjoy it."
>
> I often wonder why I enjoy participating in an AJSS project. In the middle of the summer when all of us are freaked out and really need that four day trip to Winnipeg, I'm sure it's because I'm crazy. My children enjoy it, but they also have to do things because that's the way the group voted. And they go to sleep late, and they're overtired. and they get sick. "Who needs it?" I say.

At other times I think I do it for purely selfish reasons. It costs no money. In fact, I even get paid a little to do it. I get to see the United States. I don't just pass through; I really get to know a community.

I can still feel it in my guts, those experiences. The ragged beauty of New Mexico and the nauseous feeling as we watched the Navajo woman slaughter her own sheep and helped her cook the meat. We ate it because it was part of the Navajo way of life to raise sheep for their own food. But we were almost vomiting as we ate. The first taste of dust in South Dakota, a taste which lasted throughout the summer. The faces of Mt. Rushmore – what does that chiseled out mountain have to do with America? The Indians who in their bitterness (The older ones still remembered the battle of Wounded Knee) said, "Go home, we don't need you!" And the friendly Chippewa Indians of Cloquet, Minn. where we built a community center amid the beautiful Minnesota pine trees, a center used until last summer when it was burned down. How about Crow Agency, Montana, where we lived in a small house and got on each other's nerves and the Indian teenagers slept all day and yelled outside our window all night? Then I really thought I was crazy to be there. And crazy to be in Clinton, Kentucky in a house falling down around us with the humidity so high that our clothes always smelled and when we walked into town in the morning the men were sitting around the town square shooting at blackbirds and their cars had the sign, "Register communists, not guns."

I remember the humidity of Abbeville, Louisiana, but more than that I remember the Spanish moss dripping from the trees and the Cajun French accents and the spicy Creole food and a Dominican nun whom the black people called an angel, helping them in every way after she was fired as a VISTA worker community organizer. But what I remember most about Louisiana was the day we arrived. The black community held a special prayer service to bless our project. The temperature was at least 100 degrees and the humidity almost that high. And we sat for an hour or more listening to prayers and the "Amen, yes Lords" of the people. Then we were whisked away to the home of one of the wealthiest men in town where his family and friends relaxed around the swimming pool, and I was so dumbfounded by the contrast between the prayers of the poor black people we had come to help and the insensitivity of these people who could have helped, that I spoke to no one for the rest of the afternoon. There was the summer in Iowa with its cornfields as far as one could see. And in Bluffton, Ohio and Crookston with nothing much to recommend the towns. Quiet, slow towns, flat countryside. But friendly people to recommend them. And the weeping birch trees of Crookston.

People in New York City are very provincial. They think that New York is the world. They don't understand anything else. So I may be crazy but look what I have learned and experienced. People and places aren't all the same. Our country has many accents and tastes and smells and visual impacts.

In my selfishness I've had a variety of experiences in different parts of the country. But what have I contributed? I haven't painted or hammered or put down flooring. I haven't even gotten to know the people in those homes where you've done those things. And I haven't spent as much time with the group as you've spent with each other. But I've taken part in seeing that the project runs smoothly, that you have food to eat and mail from home. And a myriad of other details that go by unnoticed. In seeing your gratification at the end of the day as you drag yourselves back to the school, I gain satisfaction. As I observe each person grow in understanding and in being able to cope with living together and working together so concentratedly, I have a good feeling that I've done my share in helping all those families that you're helping. But I still say to you and to my friend that I do it because I like it and I gain from it and not because anyone can look at me and say, "Isn't it wonderful what you're doing and aren't these people whom you're helping lucky?"

I wonder who gains more and grows more: you, the campers, or the people we're helping, or I?[25]

In addition to solidifying the operation of the campers by recruiting project directors dedicated to its central spirit, the AJSS modernized its off season activities. Though still a small operation, the New York office has expanded beyond the law offices of Henry Kohn. After an emergency operation to remove a kidney in 1953, Kohn decided that he needed to shore up the organizational structure. Although the Board of Directors has always been an informal gathering which meets in October and April, the former to review the summer projects and the latter to plan the upcoming ones, Kohn has broadened those responsible for the group's off-season activities beyond himself. In 1970 he took the position as Chairman of the Board, turning over the title of President to Michael Mayer, one of the original Kohn friends who met in his apartment to found the society.[26] The job of President is mainly that of an official set of ears for Kohn to discuss policy with, but the current President, former camper Larry Green, has recently thrown himself into an ambitious campaign to secure the financial future of the AJSS well into the new century.[27]

The job of Executive Director was also permanently established in 1971. Recruitment of campers and counselors and communication with parents both before and during the summer are the main responsibilities of this officer. Elly Saltzman held the position until 1994. Today Carl and Audrey Brenner share it.

Fifty years from its founding, the organization still has no full-time employees nor a five-day-a-week office. There is no bureaucracy promoting its own growth. Henry Kohn's law office staff and a skeletal AJSS office (with a single part-time secretary aiding the Brenners) continue to handle most of the relatively few secretarial and bookkeeping responsibilities.

Recruitment is more difficult than for a traditional summer camp. Not only is there no camp property; volunteers are expected to enroll without knowing where in the country they are headed and with no housing established until long after volunteers are committed to their summer. While most summer camps encourage recruits to bring along friends, the AJSS prefers to send friends to different sites, so that no prior attachments will interfere with the bonding of the new group. In addition, most camps center their recruitment campaigns on their returning campers, but AJSS policy is to allow each volunteer to spend only one summer between the sophomore and senior years in high school on a project, so that every year the organization needs a completely new slate of volunteers. The society has recently adopted the newest promotional approach. One may find AJSS on the internet at www.ajss.org.

Kohn still selects the hosts. In January he contacts each state's director of non-profit organizations and asks that descriptions of AJSS operations be passed on to likely sponsors. When interested parties are found, discussions about the necessities for a project – consistent work, appropriate housing, and access to transportation – winnow the field considerably. Once likely programs are selected, May visits by project directors solidify the arrangements. On several occasions, last minute cancellations by apparent hosts have forced Kohn to move quickly to substitute another project.

The development of the nation's transportation network has greatly impacted the summer experience. In the early days Henry Kohn sent telegrams to the campers directing them to a Penn Station train or a Port Authority bus for day-long journeys to their destinations. The bus ride to Frogmire, South Carolina took 22 hours.[28] Today, with airplane travel hardly more expensive than ground transportation, the campers invariably arrive at their destination through the air. Though much more convenient, some of the bonding that the longer trips created must wait until the campers have arrived, especially because smaller localities are often serviced by propeller aircraft seating nine or 18 people, and it is often impossible to have the group arrive together.

The project directors, too, arrive by plane, usually a day or two before their charges. The establishment of this practice ended a twenty year pattern of the supervisors piloting their own cars into new territory. For their initial season as directors, the Kopelowitzes drove to Abbeville, Louisiana in their yellow Volkswagon. The trip took four or five days and the novice directors were spooked by the "machine gun" above them, which turned out to be their tarpaulin flapping on the roof.[29]

Although participants arrive through the air, automobile use – usually in the form of 15 passenger vans – has vastly expanded the summer's activities. A myriad network of highways and byways has conquered the vastness of the United States, and AJSS campers spend a great deal of time traveling these roads. Only rarely, as in McAllen, Texas in 1997, does the contingent live on the work site; vehicles bring campers to work in rides ranging between ten minutes and an hour. The longer rides may be necessary because the group is working in several locations, or because the roads must avoid such scenic obstacles as the Sierra Nevadas.[30] Sometimes the routes themselves turn into dusty dirt roads, navigable at speeds no greater than five miles per hour.

Though a six week stay in any locality immerses the group in each site's unique characteristics, America's road culture produces a numbing surface sameness. The cities and towns all feature shopping malls; the larger the urban center, the larger the mall. Inside the concrete and glass, the visitor is anywhere in America; malls in Montgomery, Alabama; Atlanta, Georgia; Portland, Oregon; Boise, Idaho; McAllen, Texas; Casper, Wyoming; and Green Bay, Wisconsin are so similar that without prior knowledge the traveler might be anywhere. Malls in the south seem slightly more elaborate, perhaps a concession to the urgent need to get out of the heat. The scramble for parking outside the McAllen emporia is telling testimony to the desperate desire for ample air conditioning. So ubiquitous is the mall culture in Montgomery (the city is literally surrounded by shopping plazas), that the visitor realizes that the famous bus boycott, if held in the 1990s, would have been a failure: no one relies on buses, and there is no commercial downtown!

The road culture does not discriminate between heroes or the past and present: When a visitor travels to Montgomery, an aura of the surreal marks the awareness that one is at the intersection of boulevards named for Jefferson Davis and Rosa Parks.

Urban centers, large and small, are surrounded by a modern blight. Welcoming all car traffic from every direction are the fast food chains. Towns with fewer than 10,000 people manage to support McDonald's, Burger King, Wendy's, Kentucky Fried Chicken, Pizza Hut, Domino's, Hardee's, Subway, and dozens of other on-the-move food establishments. Instantly recognizable from the signs that constitute the unsightly skyline in villages and along the highway (and from lavish television advertising), these establishments are familiar and welcoming to teenagers from the northeast, especially those with legendary appetites that are only momentarily appeased by full-course meals and those who chafe at kosher-style dining requirements. The character of thousands of towns is swallowed up by the homogenizing impact of the fast-food population explosion. A traveler passes through miles of such landmarks, intermingled with dozens of familiarly named motels before reaching downtown. Many times the so-called central district is empty.

More often than not the principal enemy of a flourishing downtown shopping district, where individual stores once contributed to the character of the community, are two massive concrete edifices, normally placed just before or after the signs welcoming automobile traffic to town. Frequently K-Mart and Wal-Mart face each other across four or six lanes of paved tar; virtually always Wal-Mart is the victor in the discount wars, proven by the full parking lot in front.

These stores are frequented by project directors inexpensively purchasing start-up requirements like curtains for school windows, posterboard and markers to make the six-week calendar, pens and pads for use by the committees, and film,

film, and more film to record progress at work and gorgeous vistas visited. But the teenagers adore Wal-Mart, too. They enjoy their air-conditioned Mecca of all-purpose low-cost shopping. They buy packages of socks and underwear, discount bags of candy, blow-up chairs to place in their bedrooms, and absurd weekly supermarket tabloids to poke fun at. Without leaving the store they can gulp down late-night fries and a shake.

If the familiar malls, fast-food chains, motels, and giant discount emporia create an initial impression that the whole nation is merely the same place endlessly multiplied, project directors enlist education and recreation committees to counter with an immersion in the unique occupations, customs, and vistas of each site. As a priority second only to the work and its meaning as living prophetic Judaism, AJSS leaders seek to have their charges return home with a sense of what is special about the corner of America where they have spent time.

Campers in the mid-west have toured steel factories and automobile assembly plants; in the south they have attended – and participated in – the spirited sessions of black Baptist churches. In the west they have cheered on cowboys and cowgirls demonstrating skill in rodeo competition; throughout small-town America, they have watched pick-up trucks on gigantic wheels climb atop and crush old sedans. Putting on their heaviest work boots, they have waded through "cow paddies" to see and touch what will soon become the beef they eat (and to learn that the difference between veal and beef is a matter of a few months. Beef cattle do not live long lives.). In agricultural Maine, they have pulled up potato plants in July to see the coin-sized spuds that will grow to mature vegetables in a few months. For fun, they have toured long-closed spartan prisons and momentarily shut themselves in; for grim education they have seen real prisoners in modern jails. They have attended ethnic festivals and celebrated local centennials and sesquicentennials.[31]

AJSS volunteers have invited agricultural agents who explain local farming, and they have practiced irrigation on western farms. They have heard factory managers and union representatives and toured closed gold mines and working iron mines. Local ministers and rabbis have spoken before them and invited them to participate in services. Attending a local synagogue – often the only synagogue – and seeing the small size of local congregations is useful education for the New Yorker who unconsciously assumes that "almost everyone" is Jewish. In Presque Isle, Maine, one of the handful of local Jews – a Bronx expatriate – opened up the tiny, pretty synagogue and displayed the Torah while two campers blew the shofar. Normally, the temple is only opened on the High Holy Days.[32]

Campers hear about the history of their project hosts and invite those providing other social services to explain their mission. They have heard Planned Parenthood representatives explain the difficulty of work in fiercely anti-abortion communities; they have visited teenagers living in a loving foster home operated by Catholic Charities and listened to a social worker from a battered women's shelter. They have toured army, navy and air force bases and been addressed by those fighting immigration restrictions on Mexican farm workers.

Even the smallest towns have museums which record the history and the way of life of their localities. AJSS volunteers tour them and attend minor league baseball games (The quality of the play is much worse, but the interaction is splendidly intimate. There are also more activities for the bored or five-year-old fan to do). They have heard state and national wildlife officials describe and display the lifestyle of indigenous creatures and discuss the problems of human interaction. A Michigan wildlife representative stunned the romantic sensibilities of the 1999 Marquette volunteers by dubbing deer "cute rats."

When the groups visit larger cities, project directors insist on visits to art and science museums and accede to the wishes of their charges to attend the amusement park. Campers have been to Disney World and Six Flags – but it's the water parks with their immersion in relief from summer heat that provide the most fun. With the exception of New York there is not a major city in the United States that AJSS groups have not toured; a trip to the Big Apple would be redundant for these campers. Groups in Texas have visited Monterrey and Mexico City; groups in the north have been to Vancouver, Winnipeg, Toronto, Montreal, and Quebec City. That walled metropolis, perched hundreds of feet atop the St. Lawrence River and dotted with festive and quaint downtown shops, may be the prettiest city in North America.

Still, it is the natural beauty of the United States that project directors, counselors, and campers have treasured most about their weekend activities. Volunteers have walked the Appalachian Trail in Cumberland and Shenandoah Forests in Virginia and West Virginia ("Who will ever forget our hike along the Appalachian trail to that beautiful secluded waterfall?" wrote Marty and Rochelle Kopelowitz of their stay in Shenandoah[33]) or in the Berkshires in Massachusetts; they have seen the North Atlantic crash into the base of Cadillac Mountain in Acadia National Park or walked on boardwalks through marshes containing hundreds of alligators in Everglades National Park. They have seen gigantic stalactites and stalagmites and other geologic formations in scores of caverns throughout the country. They have climbed and looked at America's mightiest peaks in Rocky Mountain, Yellowstone, Grand Teton and Glacier National Parks, stared into and hiked down the Grand Canyon, and admired the desert architecture of Dinosaur and Bryce National Parks.

AJSS participants have watched the beauty of sunsets at Big Bend National Park in Texas and over the bayous of Louisiana, marveling over the vivid colors.[34] They have gaped at the stone canyons and giant sequoias of Yosemite. There they have hidden food from bears, but so have campers at Washington State's Mt. Rainier and Custer State Park in South Dakota. Marty Kopelowitz recalls the thunderstorms over the Dakota plains as being "absolutely ferocious."[35] Yellowstone – America's own animal safari – has offered members of several work projects close encounters with moose, elk, bison and smaller wildlife. Boats on Puget Sound have taken them whale watching; Jonathan Hirsh remembers the pod of Orcas off the San Juan Islands, suddenly jumping out of the water in dance formation as the group sat, stunned.[36] Volunteers have sunbathed and ocean-dipped at nationally or state protected beaches in Acadia in Maine, on islands off of the Carolinas, on the Florida Gold Coast and at Corpus Christi on the Gulf of Mexico, and on the black sands of Oregon on the Pacific. In Texas, unshaded sand was too hot to touch; in Oregon, campers wore sweatshirts and light jackets as they rode horses through wind-created ripples and small dunes.

The beauty of lakes has refreshed eyes and bodies. Jonathan Hirsh recalls the majesty of Lake Tahoe, with its near freezing temperatures and snow-capped surrounding mountains, as campers peered through clear depths to lake bottom.[37] 32,000 square miles of clean, scenic Lake Superior awed 1999 upper Michigan campers. And Crater Lake in Oregon, visited by several projects, is simply not believable: The visitor must climb up the crater before heading down to the water; there the depth of the blue color seems created by one of Hollywood's Technicolor artists rather than truly a work of nature.

Sometimes groups are fortunate to discover a local guide who will expose them to spectacular sights they would not have known. The 1998 Wyoming volunteers, already returning awed from Grand Teton Park, stopped to rendezvous with Rabbi Harry Levin, former AJSS camper and now the owner of a small ranch beside the magnificent Wind River Mountains (the local name for the Rockies in Wyoming). Meeting them at a lovely state picnic ground, Levin led the contingent upwards from the 6500 foot elevation of the starting point through snow-covered ground until they arrived, breathless from the climb, at aptly named Jade Lake. The pure turquoise of the water was enough to take the breath away – again.

Not infrequently AJSS travelers stumble on scenes of nature that surprise them. Driving deep into the Sawtooth National Forest, the 1996 Idaho group found no open campsites, but were assured they could pull off the road to raise their tents. At an elevation higher than 8000 feet above sea level, the contingent set-up camp. Surrounded by tall pines and a clear night, some forsook the shelter of tents to stare at the stars on tarps until they fell asleep. At 8 AM, as the first of them awoke, the car thermometer registered 29 degrees, a number confirmed by the frozen dew visible on tarps and sleeping bags. Descending 2000 feet, campers donned wetsuits for white water rafting. By midday the temperature had risen to 90 – and campers had learned that the Sawtooths often register the coldest temperatures in the nation.

The Pacific Northwest has provided several sets of project directors with their favorite scenic settings. Of her project in Oregon, Audrey Brenner writes:

> Our camp was located in Mt. Angel, Oregon, which is situated between the Coastal range and the Cascade range. The Willamette valley between the two is truly a Garden of Eden. Every conceivable fruit is grown there. The valley is fertile and lush. A vivid memory of ours is our campers working alongside the Benedictine Monks and Sisters, gathering fruit of all sorts using a cherry picker to pick the fruit high on the trees. One could not get closer to nature.[38]

Jules and Julianne Hirsh's 1974 project in Tacoma, Washington labored under the picturesque shadow of Mt. Rainier. The majestic peak is visible a hundred miles away; its snow-capped top and glacial crevices never lose their white cover. It was inevitable that the group would visit, but no one could have anticipated how they would view the state's best known natural landmark. National Guard General Buchanan, who had provided for all of the group's transportation needs, had the group tour the mountain from above, in helicopters. Having seen the legendary landmark in the distance for weeks, AJSS volunteers were astonished and inspired by their unique vantage point.[39]

When Marty and Rochelle Kopelowitz took their Spokane group to Rainier, they came more traditionally, using cars and vans. As they approached the snowline, the Kopelowitzes carried and cajoled their 18-month-old daughter up a few hundred feet. Playing in the snow in summer is always delicious. The family fully enjoyed the outing, and when they returned to warmer ground, they were astonished to find their daughter had intense sunburn, as the bright sunlight reflected off of the snow had done fast work.[40]

My 1994 group in Eugene, Oregon camped every weekend. We passed through the Coastal Mountains to arrive at windy, cool Oregon beaches for our first trip. The next four weekends were excursions into the glacier-etched Cascades. The first of these was pursued relaxing at Suttle Lake and climbing on and around the Sisters, three closely grouped glacial peaks. The one urban day was set in pretty Portland. The independent bookstore, Powell's, with stacks of little-known books and the coffee and snack bar which has since been imitated by retailing giants Barnes & Noble and Borders, was a highlight of our brief stay. But this group was more interested in nature, so we pushed on, driving alongside the Columbia River. At the Bonneville Dam volunteers watched the salmon swim upstream through windowed locks and then camped at the foot of mighty Mt. Hood.

The final weekends were spent at the two Cascade National Parks, Rainier and Crater Lake. Each weekend seemed more fulfilling than the last. Four Shabbat services were held in the awesome Cascade background. The group felt that the beauty of their surroundings created a fitting ambiance for the purposefulness of their work.

Many years earlier, Audrey Brenner had felt the same connection. Remembering a trip of her 1976 New Mexico group, she writes:

> In an attempt to get an early start on a weekend trip, we left our living quarters mid-day Friday. We arrived at White Sands National Monument, New Mexico, in time to set up camp and prepare for the Shabbat dinner. By the time the meal was concluded, it had begun to get dark and the sky was brilliant with a full moon and an astonishing blanket of stars. Nothing could have been more breathtaking than watching our group conduct their Shabbat service in this setting. At the end of the service, one or two of the campers led the group in Israeli

dances, while some played the guitar. The entire scene over the silky white sand and the elongated shadows of our campers dancing is a vision that we will never forget.[41]

Much has changed in the United States and in American Jewry since the organization was founded in 1950. By living the spirit of prophetic Judaism, by searching for the essential uniqueness of each locality, and by exploring the natural beauty of the land, AJSS groups search for a meaningful and enduring experience to enrich their summers and their lives.

Epilogue: Lives of Service

How does one measure the impact of the fifty years and 120 projects conducted by the American Jewish Society for Service? There is the physical evidence: hundreds of homes built and thousands more painted or renovated; scores of structures – damaged, dangerous or unsightly – demolished. Community centers, schools, parks, playgrounds, and fences have been built or improved across the nation.

But there are achievements that cannot be arithmetically approximated. From Cloquet, Minnesota, to Abbeville, Louisiana, AJSS projects have bridged gulfs between local governments and those previously not represented and between the mightiest individuals and the previously ignored powerless. "The presence of the [1980] AJSS work camp in Goldsboro [North Carolina]," wrote project host Geneva Hamilton, "improved the attitude of all racial groups. Since 1980 race relations have improved generally and we're doing more things together. Perhaps the greatest improvement is between the white and Jewish community. Some of the whites have apologized for their attitude before the program."[1]

Sister Anne Catherine Bizalion similarly declared:

> I am only too happy to have this opportunity to testify that the three summers we had the good fortune to benefit from the campers' presence were a positive experience for our communities. Particularly, the presence of AJSS brought some attention to the existence of the rather small Jewish community living here and to its contribution to the well being of our area.
>
> The campers who took part in the program were dedicated, hard working, intelligent young people, functioning well through a well organized group. The leaders have always been very sensitive to the local situations [when] acting as facilitators between the campers and the local community, and also between the different groups of the local community. They always coordinated their action with ours to bring about more understanding.[2]

In Harpswell, Maine, the activities of the AJSS group "changed the attitudes and created an ecumenical atmosphere,"[3] according to Joseph Jefferson of the Hinckley Home School Farm.

The labor of volunteers has encouraged those who felt hopeless to lift their own arms and reclaim a place in the sun, as was manifest when the Four

Corners community rebuilt their community center after the devastation of Hurricane Andrew.

From the vantage point of the AJSS spiritual founders, even more significant than the organization's impression on the world would be its impact on the volunteers themselves. Could a summer's work to aid the disadvantaged transform those who volunteered?

Every year the AJSS brochure prints anonymous comments abstracted from the project newsletters. The enthusiasm of the remarks hints at broad changes in perspective.

Here a few comments following the summer of 1999:

> The pure satisfaction I get when I build these houses is the most heart-warming thing I have ever done; it is as if I saved a life. The people I have lived with have also changed my life. . . They have modeled me into something that I was not before, and I feel it is because of them that this has been the best experience of my life.

> *   *   *

> I have watched no less than five houses arise from cold slabs of concrete and gnarled two-by-fours. These houses – soon to become homes – will bring a stable environment for children to mature in. . . Our own skills have grown and diversified, from simple framing and dry walling to insulating, sheathing, trussing and roofing. As our skills matured and the raw material began to form structures faintly resembling buildings, so too have the raw personalities of our group coalesced into a tightly bound and energetic whole.

> *   *   *

> I have never felt so content at the end of a day as I do here; I know when I go to sleep that I packed everything I could into my day, and it feels great. We have helped enrich the lives of the people in this community, and enriched our own lives in the process. We put up walls that are the foundation for a family's memories, but we also took down walls that were equally important. We took down the walls around ourselves.

> *   *   *

> All that I thought I was doing was helping build houses for low-income people. In reality I was helping build lives for these people.[4]

It is too early to know if the commitment to service expressed by these young people will illuminate their adult lives. A broader view may be possible through an examination of older veterans of AJSS summers. Here are the stories of four who have dedicated their lives to public service.

Swirling winds blew soot-filled snow onto the steps of the Governor's mansion in Albany one cold morning early on in the administration of George Pataki. Within two weeks an incinerator located in the heart of Arbor Hill, a poor black neighborhood, was closed down. For twelve years the New York State Office of General Services had run the incinerator, and public officials had ignored the complaints of community residents that the visible residue belched out by the facility contained dangerously high levels of lead. Years of frustration induced the Arbor Hill Concerned Citizens Association to seek the aid of the National Resource Defense Council in finding legal remedies. The community organization wanted more than the incinerator's closure; organizers wanted active steps taken to remedy the pollution ingested by residents for half a generation. Even after the proximity of the dangerous substance had induced state officials to end years of intransigence, bureaucrats were still ignoring claims for restoration, claiming there was no proof the closed plant was the source for high levels of lead in the air.

Litigators for the NRDC took a two-level approach in negotiating with state officials. While threatening to sue the state, they realized this was an uncertain prospect because the current Hazardous Waste Law makes the litigant prove "imminent and substantial endangerment to health or the environment." The NRDC would have to prove the lead came from the incinerator, instead of any other source. Nonetheless, a suit would have been an embarrassing prospect for a newly proclaimed "environmental" governor. The environmental lawyers also suggested it was politically savvy for the administration to settle. As the incinerator was built during the days of Democrat Mario Cuomo, the responsibility for the disaster might be shunted onto the opposition party, while the current governor could earn clean air credentials. The state agreed to a settlement of $1.4 million, which the Arbor Hill residents have used in two ways. Most of the funds will establish a community based environmental and technology center in the neighborhood to educate residents about the dangers of lead. The remainder will be used for abatement of contaminated sites. Though the settlement was not perfect, as the funds allocated were not sufficient to undo all of the damage, it was satisfying that the complaints of the community organization were heard and addressed by a state government which had ignored the peril for twelve long years.

NRDC attorney Nancy Marks took particular pleasure in the empowerment of the Arbor Hill Concerned Citizens Association. Her long career as an environmental lawyer has brought her many victories, but few bring such vivid reminders of her earliest introduction to a community organization struggling for its just grievances to be addressed despite governmental indifference or hostility.

In Abbeville, Louisiana, Marks spent the summer of 1971 renovating housing and installing indoor plumbing as she and her fellow AJSS campers helped Sister Anne Catherine Bizalion and the Southern Mutual Help Association force the city to recognize that Rabbit Hill was their responsibility.

Young Nancy had heard about the AJSS from her cousin, Gary Ekman, who had gone to Seaford, Delaware with Jules and Julianne Hirsh in 1970. Originally she had wanted to go to Oregon, but her cousin convinced her she would learn more in Louisiana, so she made that her first choice. She was appalled by the indifference of the local churches to the miserable poverty of the black residents and affirms Jules Hirsh's claim that the AJSS's presence made local churches and politicians realize it was better to help than to ignore the problem. She still remembers work supervisor Murphy Wright as an extraordinary man. "Murph was an amazing guy, the kind of a person you meet once in a lifetime." Murphy Wright was a pastor; this was "the first time I had a positive view of the church. He commanded respect." Here was a minister climbing on the roof to repair houses. She remembers that they "built bridges over sewers." One memorable day campers were asked by the homeowner if they wanted some root beer. "It had never occurred to us" that she would spend money on them .the volunteers had answered "sure" without knowing the soda wasn't already there. When they realized the homeowner had used her own food stamps to buy them drinks, they felt guilty.

Abbeville gave young Nancy Marks a consciousness of power, racism and government oppression or indifference. "This helps me represent clients. I think about it more now than twenty years ago." In Abbeville, "I was very idealistic and cynical – idealistic about doing good and cynical about the way the government works."

By the time of her AJSS summer, Nancy had already been politically involved; she'd been "Clean for Gene" McCarthy in 1968. But she wasn't political in college, where she concentrated her effort as a geology major at Williams. She was not enamored of the school. It was beautiful and she liked the austere country setting, but she didn't like the "preppy-cocktail party-lacrosse" crowd. Still, she loved all her courses. "I was interested in everything." She began going to graduate school in geology at Stanford, but something was missing. Though she still found the subject matter fascinating, she soon dropped out and "floundered." She worked at a national park and as a carpenter in California. The physical labor once again helped her find direction. Realizing she wanted to have a political job, she enrolled in Harvard Law School in 1980 to become a public interest environmental lawyer. Her public interest career could have taken any direction, but the young idealist felt it made most sense to take advantage of her background in science, especially as her scientific curiosity never left her. Before her graduation in 1983 she had met her husband, a colleague at Harvard.

When she graduated she worked as an unpaid legal fellow at the National Resource Defense Council in San Francisco for a year. Her job was to prepare suits against the United States government about offshore oil slicks. The NRDC charged that federal policy allowed the oil companies to misuse the coast to exploit the environment. The oil companies were buying leases off the coastline for virtually no money and providing no environmental guarantees. She also fought ranchers who were involved in the "desert-ification" of public lands by grazing animals and destroying parkland, while being provided government subsidies.

Having gotten her environmental feet wet, Marks returned to Boston to work for the Massachusetts Attorney-General's environmental protection division. At that time, this was "an office with a mission." Encouraged to discover environmental outlaws, she sued polluters. Most often the small firms would pay a fine and settle without a trial. "For a government agency it was pretty good." Her husband began teaching law at Rutgers in Newark. She almost took a job working for the state of New Jersey litigating against those who pollute the wetlands, but she was offered a position at the NRDC. She has worked in the New York office since 1987, suing water polluters as part of the Citizens Enforcement Project. As in Boston, most of the firms settle on the eve of trial, paying money and promising clean-ups. Then the NRDC watches to ensure no polluter recidivism. Some firms have faced several NRDC suits.

Her favorite target has been Texaco. In 1988 she won her fifth case against the oil giant for trashing the Delaware River. Though the Citizen's Enforcement Project is no longer in operation, the activist attorney has just boxed another round with Texaco. Ordered years ago to clean up the Delaware, the oil firm didn't; instead the corporation issued a bogus study, which declared there was nothing wrong in the river. The NRDC exposed it as being a fraud; the judge interposed and told Texaco to either conduct a thorough investigative study, verifiable by independent observers, or face a heavy fine. The suspicion is that the sediments in the river are toxic.

Another oil company antagonist was Arco-Alaska. In the fabled North Slope the firm was drilling for oil and storing the mineral in unsecured above-ground pits; Marks' intervention has forced the company to clean up. She has compelled corporate polluters Bethlehem and Upjohn to pay substantial penalties. Suspicious of the large firms, she has enjoyed litigating against them. Marks is uncomfortable with the Clintonian collaborative model. "I don't trust them [the large corporations] to do the right thing. By law their job is to maximize profits."

Today she works on a "litigation swat team." They "pick intractable problems that won't get resolved." Along with the federal government, the NRDC is suing American Electric Power for illegally extending the life of dirty, old coal-fired power plants in Ohio. Many local governments are involved, but the NRDC is representing people affected by the local pollution. "At stake is billions of dollars in savings for the companies [if they can avoid cleaner gas-powered furnaces] and billions of tons of pollutants." The old power plants are supposed to be phased out, but instead American Electric has been stealthily upgrading the coal-powered plants which must adhere to older and easier regulations. If unstopped, the company will have frustrated the intent of the law to eliminate coal-powered plants in 30 years. Instead these carbon monoxide producers will still be heating the atmosphere for another 60. The NRDC seeks huge penalties and gas-powered furnaces.

The great difference between the Citizen's Enforcement Project and her current work is that today either community groups seek out Marks and her colleagues or she finds them. Community empowerment – so vital in Abbeville and in Albany – is at the root of a current project. The Maine People's Alliance suspects the greatest level of mercury poisoning in the food chain anywhere can be found in that state's waterways. The federal government is forcing clean-up just around the area of the plants, but contamination runs all through the river and its wildlife. The NRDC suit is demanding that Mallincrodt, the firm responsible for most of the pollution, conduct a thorough study and then prepare a comprehensive plan of restoration.

Marks tries for inventive use of environmental laws – to "push the envelope" on them; now she's looking for a case involving the health of workers. She looks forward to working with a union or workers' organization which would allow her to aid the empowerment of people too long victimized. "The work I do is consistent. I would never be a lawyer in the other context. I'll never make as much as a first year associate in a New York law firm. It's not the relevant comparison."

One of 180 employees in four offices on both coasts, Marks enjoys her work in a mainstream environmental group with a diversity of political views. An organizational gadfly, she's opposed to accepting corporate funding. The NRDC takes small amounts from firms with progressive reputations, like Patagonia and Ben and Jerry's. Even this makes Marks uneasy, since she prefers less money and more independence. But her integrity is respected by her colleagues. "There's a role for people like me."[5]

The cherished hope of Isidor Hoffman, Ferdinand Isserman, and Arthur Lelyveld was that the American Jewish Society for Service would be a vehicle to transmit the spirit of living Judaism – a belief Jews must act against inequity - to the young people who enrolled in its projects. It would be foolish to insist that all of those who have participated have had their lives transformed. Six or seven weeks, even if they constitute "the best summer of my life," do not guarantee a metamorphosis.

Yet everyone who has gone has widened horizons. Virtually all of the volunteers have been exposed to physical labor, social classes, and a corner of the United States they might never have known. If all that emerged from the summer were these memories, each would have become a broadened human being. Stephen Killian, who was a camper in Fort Duchesne, Utah in 1968 and one of Nancy Marks' counselors in Abbeville, is now practicing family medicine in Annapolis. He feels grateful that he "was exposed to communities, cultures, and work experiences that were to remain truly unique in my life. I will forever treasure those memories."[6]

Evidence of substantial impact on hundreds of lives abounds. Scores of families have made an AJSS summer a mandatory rite of passage. Brothers, sisters, cousins, and children (and soon, grandchildren) await their summer, their moment of attesting to their Judaism with service to others. For many, AJSS service projects are proving grounds for the establishment of a humanitarian ethos, proof that life offers them, as it has Nancy Marks, "a role for people like me."

Many of these campers, frustrated by the one summer only rule, seek out service projects with their AJSS summer host organization or go abroad to continue their service. Rachel Cane, who built the community center destroyed by Hurricane Andrew in 1992, returned to the Southern Mutual Help Association, where she "spent a year in our office constructing a development plan and creating an orderly archival system for us. She truly established a foundation upon which our own endowment can begin to build. Her help was invaluable... she has left a wonderful legacy behind."[7]

Campers have "graduated" from the AJSS and entered the Peace Corps. Janna Cohen-Rosenthal found that her experience in McAllen, Texas in 1997 meant that she needed to spend a year between high school and college to do "social action work" in Israel.[8] Many AJSS counselors are former campers or their siblings. Elizabeth "Sack" Brody spent the difficult summer of 1956 in Winsted, Connecticut, but her enthusiasm propelled her son Richard, now a rabbinical student, to be a counselor for the 1993 El Paso project.[9]

Some AJSS graduates have found that the message of service resonates throughout their lives. 1995 Tulsa counselor Michael Steele writes that "community service is still an integral part of my life and a fantastic way to broaden one's perspective," which in his case means pursuit of a master's degree in social work.[10] Similarly, Michael Kaplan, a 1978 volunteer in Hattiesburg, Mississippi, declares that his "one summer as a camper and two as a counselor left indelible marks on the development of my character, career choices and sense of myself in relation to community. As with others involved in AJSS, it changed my life." Kaplan is a child psychiatrist on the faculty of the Yale Child Study Center.[11]

Ann Hirsh Greenhill, whose children and nephews and nieces all participated in AJSS summers, was herself a volunteer in Pine Ridge, South Dakota in 1963. She found that the organization "was a profound and pivotal experience for me which shaped my soul and life choices." She has "been working for 12 years for a non-profit organization coordinating respite services for families with developmental disabilities."[12]

Jane Plitt worked with the Minnesota Chippewas in 1964 and became a labor arbitrator. Her professional work has centered on securing equal rights for women. She worked to "end sex-segregated want ads in New York State," and "brought suit against the Jaycees to admit women."[13] Another reservation alumnus, Andrea Avrutis, who spent the summer of 1968 in Busby, Montana, writes that she has "supported the St. Labre Indian school, a private Catholic school on both the Cheyenne and Crow reservations for many years, based on my AJSS summer on the Cheyenne reservation... Once I knew there are hungry people with outdoor plumbing in below zero winters, I could not send my limited resources to my various alma maters, to the environment, to politics, to arts or organized religion. Maybe it's because I was on AJSS in the summer of 1968. I also try to treat all people, except the wealthy and arrogant, with respect and dignity."[14]

Julie Pulenwitz spent the summer of 1986 in Cincinnati, Ohio. Having earned a doctorate from the Harvard School of Public Health, she is now employed by the Horizons Population Council, working on "a global HIV/AIDS prevention research project." She writes, "Community service has always been an important part of my life. The manual labor I did and the homeless shelter we lived in during my summer with AJSS made me increasingly aware of the difficult situations many people experience and they influenced my decision to pursue a career in public health and HIV/AIDS prevention."[15]

     *   *   *   *   *   *   *

When the New Mexico legislature approved funding for full-day kindergarten in that state's public schools in February 2000, it was largely because of the efforts of Think New Mexico, a non-partisan think tank established by a Manhattan expatriate who had first seen the state as a 16-year-old AJSS volunteer. Fred Nathan was destined to go on an AJSS summer. His father (also Fred Nathan) was an old friend of Henry Kohn's and an original member of the organization's Board of Directors. Young Fred grew up in Manhattan with the stereotypical view that the Hudson and East Rivers were the boundaries of the important world. During the spring of 1977, there were rumors of three projects; Nathan heard one was to be in California (it never materialized; that summer other groups went to Massachusetts and Wisconsin). "If left to my own devices," he says, "I would have picked elsewhere." But when he saw the wide-open beauty of southern New Mexico, he was "mesmerized."[16]

Vista volunteer Kraig Hagood invited AJSS to "build a park and recreational facility on the grounds of the Concilio Compensino de Sudoeste, a recently constructed community center."[17] Though anti-poverty funds were already drying up, there was still grant money available from the federal government to communities below the poverty line. If a community project was approved, the local organization would supply labor and federal funds would purchase materials. When the original laboring crew backed out, VISTA called on AJSS as an emergency replacement.

Nathan regrets that the structure of the project limited his contact with the community being aided. Instead there was grim education. "We built a tool shed to lock up equipment. One morning we came back and the tool shed had been ripped off." Years later Nathan returned to San Miquel to view the park; it had been destroyed and abandoned. The lesson he learned is that anti-poverty initiatives must get the community invested; he's applied this notion in the public service career that has followed. Another frighteningly memorable day was spent in Juarez.

As Audrey and Carl Brenner put it, "Immediately upon crossing the border one is startled by the poverty and filth in comparison to the beautiful city of El Paso."[18]

One of the highlights of the summer was arranging to meet Governor Jerry Apodaca; at the time Nathan was most impressed that the governor had an autographed Dallas cowboy football. Now Apodaca is a radio talk show host in Santa Fe and Nathan enlisted him in Think New Mexico's education campaign.

Fred Nathan followed his father in pursuing a legal career, attending Northwestern University. Convinced he would practice public interest law, Nathan worked in a legal clinic and wrote a long article for the Journal of International Law and Business about Apartheid and slave labor. For a time he was convinced he would return to New York and join the district attorney's office, but during the summer of 1985 he interned for Rudy Giuliani in the federal government's southern district. "The best young attorneys worked there; they were uniformly miserable," unhappy with life in the big city and the U.S. Attorney's office. During the second summer of law school he "decided to experiment and live in a quality-of-life-type city; I wanted to avoid the old boy network, wanted to avoid the heat and I came up with Albuquerque and Santa Fe," in no small part because of his AJSS experience there (He also looked into opportunities in Seattle and Portland. He was told to avoid Seattle because there was only one major client, and he was embarking on a risky business venture: the man was Bill Gates). Fred worked for Sutin, Thayer, and Browne in a firm of 55 lawyers, huge for New Mexico. Nine of the attorneys were Jewish; they joked that if Nathan returned, "we'll have a minion." During that summer, Nathan clerked, researched, and was rewarded with an invitation to join the firm on graduation. When he accepted, his family decided, "Freddy's going through a stage; he'll be back." Nathan is more at home in New Mexico than ever.

For three years Nathan worked for Sutin, Thayer, until he was enlisted to manage the gubernatorial campaign of Attorney General Paul Bardacke. His candidate lost the election, but fellow Democrat Tom Udall, scion of a southwest political family, won as Attorney General, and he put Nathan to work as a state attorney.

This was a time of great education and accomplishment for the young lawyer. In charge of New Mexico's lawsuit against tobacco companies, Nathan participated, as a "hard-liner," in the joint negotiations with the majority of states suing the giant corporations. The suit will return $1.25 billion over the next 25 years to New Mexico, an astounding sum for that poorly funded government.

Fred also worked on landmark drunk-driving legislation; he totally rewrote and toughened the laws. In 1993 New Mexico had the highest per capita drunk driving fatalities in the nation; in two years subsequent to the new laws, driving-while-intoxicated fatalities fell 19% while nationally they fell about 1%. Now the state is third in the nation; Nathan ruefully acknowledges this may seem like small progress, but claims the figures demonstrate "how far ahead we were of every other state."

Nathan introduced pioneer legislation enabling land use reform. In his state, corruption is associated with development; in the south, developers created the aptly named *colonias* – housing with no plumbing, sewage, and/or electric facilities, often "serviced" by dirt roads. These "third world" conditions are a scandal all along the border with Mexico. In New Mexico, the county commissioners had no authority to interfere with the developers. In one horrific incident, a small child died because the road was so narrow the ambulance couldn't reach him to bring him to the hospital. Chicano youngsters were walking through sewage to get to their schools. As a result of the legislation Nathan's exposure pushed through the legislature, commissioners can require wide roads and sewage lines. While he feels a start has been made, he acknowledges there is much to do to make the *colonias* truly habitable.

When Tom Udall was elected to congress in 1998, Nathan could have continued in the Attorney General's office, but he was ready for a new challenge. Frustrated that New Mexico is listed 49 or 50 in so many national rankings, he decided the state needed a new organization.

> Think New Mexico [he wrote] was founded with the idea than an independent, solution-oriented think tank serving the citizens of New Mexico could help to advance New Mexico. . . After all, New Mexico is already the envy of many states for the quality of its people, its beautiful landcapes and its rich cultures. That is why so many people choose to live in the land of enchantment. We believe that New Mexico, with all its potential, should be leading the parade rather than following it.
>
> Our mission is to educate the public, the media and policymakers about the serious problems facing New Mexico and to inform the public dialogue by developing comprehensive, long-term solutions to these problems.
>
> Our approach is to perform and publish sound, non-partisan research. Unlike many think tanks, we do not subscribe to any particular ideology. Instead our focus is to develop effective and pragmatic solutions.[19]

Nathan began by encouraging members of both political parties to serve on Think New Mexico's board. Stuart Udall, Tom's father and a former congressman and Secretary of the Interior, agreed to serve as Chairman of the Board, which also includes a former governor, a former attorney general, a former US ambassador, Roberta Cooper Ramo, the first elected woman president of the American Bar Association, and LaDonna Harris, a member of the Commanche nation and the President of Americans for Indian Opportunity.

Under Nathan's leadership, his organization has identified four areas of concentration: education, economic development, crime, and water use.

Education seemed the obvious place to start. Nathan wanted to begin by intervening on behalf of his state's youngest citizens by focusing on early childhood education. While full day kindergarten is utilized by 55% of the eligible population nationally, New Mexico enrolls just 14.7 %. That group qualifies for federal funding; the state pays not a penny for full day kindergarten. Other five-year-olds are enrolled in 2 ½ hour daily programs. "There are children who spend more time on the bus going to kindergarten than in the classroom."

In September 1999, Think New Mexico issued a report demonstrating how full day kindergarten could increase achievement; State legislator Amy Feldman called Nathan and asked to sponsor the legislation, which was sent to the Business and Industry committee, where it died. This outcome did not surprise Fred, who says "Progressive legislation is sent there to be killed." The traditional political response, stated most authoritatively by the House speaker – "we can't afford it" - produced the think tank's second major research project. In December 1999 their study detailed how to cut government waste to pay for the funds. In addition to noting the savings to be gained by cutting the number of kindergarten bus trips in half, the report documented abuses in contracting – 11% of the state budget - to save $14 million. The study discovered that since 1943 the tax code has given tobacco companies a volume discount, today worth $500,000. Nathan's was outraged that "a tax break goes out to reward an industry that poisons thousands of New Mexicans a year."

Fred carefully cultivated relationships with New Mexico newspapers. *The Albuquerque Tribune* and *The Santa Fe New Mexican*[20] printed editorials and features touting the think tank's recommendations. This helped to turn the tide against opponents, including two other groups opposed to the initiative. The Christian Coalition "would rather see these kids home with their mommas," and the teacher's union wanted to concentrate attention on the poor salaries of educators before addressing other issues.

Think New Mexico carefully prodded business organizations to offer support with promises of a more educated work force. The organization secured an endorsement from the Association of Commerce and Industry (the state's conservative Chamber of Commerce), convincing them to spend money sponsoring legislation for the first time. Nathan and his colleagues organized parents, kindergarten teachers, the League of Women Voters, the American Association of Retired People and the Hispano Chamber of Commerce.

Eventually, it became almost politically impossible to oppose the initiative. In February 2000, full day kindergarten was enacted by state legislators by a combined vote of 91-12; the Christian coalition was appeased by allowing families an option for a half-day. The governor has "changed his position from 'hell, no' to 'no' to 'maybe' to 'probably.'" The Republican executive doesn't like the state budget; he's "threatening to veto it and we may have to start all over again. But we've proved that the model can work. Identify the problem, drain the politics, and make the solution."

On March 8, the last possible date he could do so, Governor Gary Johnson signed the legislation approving full day kindergarten. He also vetoed the budget, so while full day kindergarten is state policy, funding the program and other Think New Mexico education initiatives is the new fight. The press credited Nathan and his organization for its first achievement.[21] The energetic attorney is resolute in his decision to create a lifework of public service to the state he fell in love with the first time he committed himself to the needs of others.[22]

*   *   *   *   *   *   *

Perhaps no man has done as much to change the nature of services offered to the mentally ill and mentally retarded, both in the public schools and in publicly supported institutions, as Stanley Herr. The sheer breadth and depth of his professional life almost defies comprehension. His life of service began in Cherokee, North Carolina, as a camper with the American Jewish Society for Service.

Herr had no prior connection to AJSS. He discovered the organization in the summer camp ads at the back of the *New York Times Magazine*. His father, "a poor immigrant from Lithuania, came over in 1919 and prospered and believed in community service. [He] always had a feeling for the underdog. He believed if you could choose to be anything, you should be a humanitarian." This was the ethos that led young Herr to select a volunteer summer. He applied late, but he believes that Henry Kohn's discovery that the young man was bound for Yale "sealed" his tardy entry. He saw the AJSS founder as an inspiring model; he was impressed that Kohn's legal career gave him the opportunity for public service.

Herr believes that early strong experiences of service are formative. "The Jesuits are right: at a young age, give us the boy and we'll shape the man." His summer in Cherokee "made me seek out challenges where I could apply ethics in a real world way. I saw that I liked working with people of different cultures and socio-economic classes and learned I could be empathetic." The AJSS gave him a sense he could be some kind of a leader. He discovered that "Jewish identity was more than lox and bagels and synagogue . . . We could help other communities." He particularly savored defying the worst expectations of the Indians. Experiences with religious sects led the Cherokees to anticipate proselytizing, but the Jewish organization wanted to help, not to convert.

As with many AJSS volunteers, Herr's experience led him to seek additional service. During the summer of 1964, he worked with the International Voluntary Service in Switzerland, building mountain roads for the relatively poor Romansch speaking villagers of Switzerland, in order to combine his "desire for adventure and travel with helping others." For eight weeks young Herr swung pick and shovel, building a road over the Alps.

During his undergraduate years, he became active in student politics. He joined the Americans for Review of Far Eastern Policy, mentored by Allard

Lowenstein and Norman Thomas. The group advocated diplomatic relations with China and an end of the Vietnam war. He was a leader of an effort to collect 2000 signatures among the Yale community for an ad in the *New York Times* against the war. Writing his senior thesis for his interdisciplinary major in sociology and politics enabled him to continue with his political and public service orientation. The title was *Community Action in the Negro Neighborhood* and he conducted his research in the central wards of Newark, studying the work of radical organizer Tom Hayden.

Herr decided to continue at Yale to pursue his law degree – an ambition since he'd been in grade school. During the 1960s, Yale had become known as a "policy" school and a place that trained a new breed of public interest lawyers. New legal theory and social approaches were being advocated. He wanted to become an "activist" attorney to remake social and political institutions and the law. He joined a weekly discussion group to bolster the idealistic students' aim to shun conventional law careers, and he was one of the founders of the *Yale Review of Law & Social Action*. Herr and his fellow editors solicited articles from legal activists outside the academy on ways that the law could be changed to benefit society. One such article was a critique of legal education by Duncan Kennedy, who later became a professor at Harvard Law School.

During a national day of protest, Herr co-led a one-day strike at Yale against the secret Cambodian bombings. During these "heady days," the young legal student held to a radical critique of the legal system and aimed at change it. He advocated the expungement of criminal records for misdemeanors – like the trespassing charges frequently used against student sit-downs. This proposal was ultimately passed by the state of Connecticut. He counseled others about avoiding the draft.

Like Fred Nathan, Stan Herr experimented with summer interning during his law school years. He spent one summer working at a prestigious Philadelphia corporate law firm. He "knew I didn't want to do that," when his superiors assigned him to develop arguments as to why part-time workers at a country club shouldn't be unionized.

The following summer he worked for New York City Mayor John Lindsay and his welfare department chief, Mitchell Ginsberg. One of the highlights was serving as the Administration's liaison to the decentralized school district in East Harlem. He was assigned to create a two-week summer camp experience for neighborhood kids; he managed to "borrow" a summer camp and begged and borrowed food and staff. The endeavor was a success, because "we brought all the kids back alive and happy."

One of his great influences at law school was Charles Reich. Reich's class, which was supposed to be in property law, read "real books" (texts detailing the inequities of contemporary society) instead of cases. From the larger group Reich selected 15 of the most promising students for a novel seminar, "Law for a New Society." Herr studied how to use legal strategies to transform Newark.

Herr's high achievement in law school gave him several opportunities to pursue. He could clerk, attend the London School of Economics, or enter public interest law. This was the "hot new place to be," and he was eager to test his legal skills on behalf of he poor. He was invited to join the new Stern Community Law Firm. Philip Stern, the Sears heir, used his foundation money to hire six lawyers, including three just emerging from law school, to develop public interest law.

Stan Herr wanted to become a children's rights lawyer and was given carte blanche to design children's rights activity. His most celebrated case developed from an unusual approach to conducting research. To discover the concerns of parents and students in the District of Columbia, the young attorney walked in the parks of the capital, asking residents what the biggest problems of the schools were. He hoped to discover if there were legal tools to correct the problems mentioned to him. He quickly unearthed a common complaint about the ills of the schools. Young children were getting thrown out of school. Discipline in 1970-1971 included little due process.

Once he discovered a cause, he needed a client among the suspended kids. He wanted to examine the behavioral and emotional reasons, often labeled "mental retardation" and "multiple disabilities," for the suspensions and test them in court. When he found a client, he had what he calls a "Eureka moment." In the neighborhood of Anacostia, "practically a third-world place," Gregory Jones, 7, hadn't been in school for three months. His mother had been told to wait for a phone call placing her son in a small classroom because he was "retarded." Why, asked Herr, was Gregory called retarded? The seven-year-old knew the reason. He threw spitballs in the classroom and called his teacher babyface. Her name was Miss Nelson. The "retarded" youngster had heard of Babyface Nelson and had applied the moniker to his teacher. Gregory had sophisticated drawings of football players and wanted to become a college football player; his mother despaired of getting her son through grade school.

Young Gregory led the way for Mills vs. the Board of Education of District of Columbia, perhaps as revolutionary for its class of victims as Brown vs. Board of Education of Topeka, Kansas. There were 2000 Gregorys in the Washington area completely out of school and many more in inappropriate settings with arbitrary classifications. If segregation was a violation of the equal protection provisions of the constitution based on race discrimination, the same was true of exclusions based on disability. The decision of 1972, the first on that subject, determined that all children have the right to an appropriate publicly supported education. The judgment led to modern special education definitions with whole new classifications for identifying, channeling and educating children with special needs.

Suddenly, Herr became "Mr. Busy." He was invited to address the Indiana legislature at the age of 27; he "waved sabers at them." They reformed their state education system without litigation. Within two years there were 32 states with the Mills type of lawsuits; Herr advised many and finally urged Congress to act. What emerged was the Education for All Handicapped Children Act, guaranteeing individuals with disabilities proper placement. The law incorporates the blueprint of process, placement, and procedures contained in the Mills decision. Congress relied on Mills and a similar case in Pennsylvania for background; later the Supreme Court would cite Mills as a legal landmark in interpreting the law.

His success made Herr a senior attorney in two years. Seeking a new challenge, he moved to the national office of the National Legal Aid and Defenders Association. Despite its impressive name, the office employed three lawyers and Herr was soon at work to help colleagues in Alabama, suing Governor George Wallace for the "warehouse conditions" of the mentally ill in state hospitals. Herr's colleague in Alabama was the local lawyer, George Dean, who was "out of central casting with big drawl and dramatic manner." He had no knowledge or expertise in the field of mental retardation. Quaint expressions like "Good morning sugar boy, we got work to do," were his stock in trade. "I would try to keep him reasonably focussed to create a federal right to treatment for the mentally ill and a right to habilitation for the mentally retarded to learn life skills."

To collect evidence, Herr ventured into "scary institutions that left their mark on my psyche to this day." He was "haunted and strangely happy that I could be using my legal skills to enter hellholes and get [victims] out." At the Partlow State School and Hospital, the typical ward had 120 people, "mostly half naked, some completely naked, milling around, some hitting heads against walls, some moaning, some bleeding, without any activity, completely idle, so that when you enter the room as a new interesting object, 100 people start coming in your direction." A legal aide to Herr wore a green outfit and miniskirt; she was "freaked out" when approached by the motley group. "Presiding over this chaos was maybe two aides, sitting in their staff room watching TV."

Herr discovered a person in seclusion who'd been there for six years. He had a coffee can for a toilet. "Needless to say his hygiene wasn't so great; his morale was worse." Herr found seclusion to be a barbaric practice which only intensified the troubles of those allegedly being helped. Partlow was beside the University of Alabama, but the feeling was of life in the medieval era. Herr was shown a treatment site, a basement where the worst behavior problems were kept. Here "aversive therapy" was practiced. Workers chased residents and zapped them with an electrified cattle prod. The attorney was told inmates didn't feel pain because they were retarded and the prods didn't give much of a jolt. He applied it to his fingertips and fell to the floor from the shock.

From this experience, Herr became the principal draftsman of treatment for the retarded. Wyatt vs. Stickney, another landmark case, was the first to hold that state institutions have obligations to uphold minimum standards for the mentally ill and mentally retarded. At the time the per capita expenditure per patient in the state institution was $3.50 a day, half the amount for animals in the Birmingham zoo.

The decision by Federal Judge Frank M. Johnson, Jr. reinforced Herr's direction. He now had two missions: to get a million kids back in school "and to do something about institutions that compared unfavorably to prisoner of war camps." Herr fought the much publicized legal battle against Willowbrook State Hospital in Staten Island, where there were 5209 people "in one god-awful place."

With these legal victories, Herr was seen as an expert, but he didn't feel like one; he wished to explore the history of treatment for the mentally ill and mentally retarded and to investigate international initiatives in the field. Awarded funding, he enrolled at the Oxford Faculty of Law to earn a Doctorate in Philosophy. Though he threw himself into the academic work (his studies commenced with investigations of ninth century English law and continued toward the modern age), Herr was too socially driven just to stick to academic concerns. "After Gregory I was driven, on a mission; I'd get impatient about things that I'd see, irritated even at Sweden." Despite the charged intellectual atmosphere at Oxford's Balliol College, he interrupted his studies to return to Washington to aid the National Legal Services Corporation, the new federal program for legal aid for the poor, in its formative days.

Herr's later career has balanced an impressive record in teaching, litigation, and study. He taught at Harvard Law School as visiting scholar, where he was awarded a fellowship to instruct lawyers to help people with mental retardation. He helped to create the Developmentally Disabled Assistance and Bill of Rights Act of 1975, which mandated that every state have an independent advocacy office that can pursue legal remedies for persons with mental retardation and related disabilities. Now there are such offices in every state. His study shaped the way the advocacy offices work. When Herr entered this field there were 205,000 people in institutions almost uniformly of abysmal quality; now there are about 65,000 in institutions and 300,000 in small group homes - a complete change from the past.

At Harvard in 1976, Herr was supposed to finish his research, but worldly issues got in the way again. Creating a clinical program to teach legal students how to represent people with mental retardation, he became an instructor. On a Rockefeller fellowship at Columbia University, Herr investigated human rights at a time when the Carter administration was creating the first US human rights policy. He found time to finish his doctorate in 1979.

Herr was recruited by the University of Maryland to develop a disability law specialty. He's enamored of the law school. "It's got all things I like; it's democratic, public, and has the highest number of blacks in a multiethnic school. It has one of the best clinical programs in the country." He has been there since 1983, working in "a pure labor of love."

From 1993 to 1995, Herr was a Kennedy Public Policy Fellow assigned to the White House Domestic Policy Council. He was one of nine professionals with broad vistas, though his specialty was disabilities and homeless issues. He had to read every bill that bore on his area and inject the administration viewpoint. Of course, sometimes this meant that Herr was creating that perspective. He substantially rewrote the federal plan dealing with cycles of homelessness. As a result of this effort, President Clinton doubled the federal budget for the homeless and extended the earned income tax credit to somewhat higher income levels. He advocated better coordination of mental health and substance abuse programs. Housing and Urban Development Secretary Andrew Cuomo took his proposals seriously. "For a federal program to double its funding in one year is unusual."

Herr was responsible for the disability aspects of Clinton's health care proposals. He regrets the failure of Congress to enact universal health benefits. Herr assessed progress made under the Americans with Disabilities Act and coordinated the ADA's fourth anniversary rally for health care. It was moving to see 2600 disabled people at the White House. "It was their house, too, and their law and their achievement; I really appreciated that sense of empowerment."

There were frustrations, too. "The gap between rhetoric and accomplishment is always nagging. Knowing that we were within arm's length of getting 40 million people health care and that we're further away is nagging."

Herr felt lucky to be a witness to the White House lawn ceremony after the Arafat-Rabin accords. At the time he wrote a memo suggesting disability cooperation between the Palestinians and Israelis.

From August 1999 to the summer of 2000, Stanley Herr was in Israel as a visiting professor at Haifa University. There he researched comparisons between Israeli and US disability anti-discrimination laws. "True to form I can't just do pure research. I spent a little time agitating because of the failure to implement the laws." [23]

Always the gadfly, Herr pushes internationally for better treatment for the disabled. In February 2000, he wrote to the Israeli press:

> Israel as a society has been reminded of the poverty of this [disabled] community and the subsistence nature of their benefits. But it has barely begun to grapple with other issues. Here's a short list of them. Accessibility to the physical environment, let alone to the mainstreams of educational, cultural, and economic life, is highly problematic. The lack of implementation of existing laws mocks even the sparse rights that are due to people with disabilities on paper. For example, the Equal Rights for People with Disabilities Law, passed in 1998 and intended to enter into force on January 1, 1999, still has no regulations, no appointed commissioners, and no systematic publicity. Its beneficiaries barely know that it is designed to remedy discrimination in the spheres of employment and transportation, let alone employers and transportation providers who will have to deliver on the law's obligations. Then there are the tensions created by widening inequalities between disabled veterans and the civilian disabled population, including those with congenital or early onset disabilities such as cerebral palsy, post-polio, and mental retardation and other chronic intellectual

disabilities. The invisibility of their problems, especially when they occur among new immigrants or the Arab sector, hampers any policy or practical solutions. In various parts of the country, the weak development (or nonexistence) of community supports for early education, least restrictive special education for those of regular school age, residential supports, and independent living condemns tens of thousands to lives of despair and over-dependence on others. Even compared to those with work-related disabilities, the ordinary Israeli with a disability is struggling to live, let alone enjoy the rights of citizenship

Israel must decide between Social Darwinism [a survival of the fittest approach] and real social rights for people with disabilities. In comparison with other social democracies with which Israel likes to compare itself, Israel lags far behind in the field of disability rights and quality-of-life realities for its 600,000 citizens with disabilities. What's to be done about their predicament? First, the government can implement the Equal Rights law now with seriousness and commitment. Second, the Knesset can fill some of the gaps by legislating further in terms of early education, nondiscrimination in public accommodations and the provision of more self-determined services and supports. Third, the disability community itself needs to organize for the long term as a dynamic and vigilant coalition. Finally, the public should remember that – given the chances of accident or illness - this is the only minority group that one might (involuntarily) join at any time. Thus, the rights that you protect may become your own or that of your children or grandchildren. One clear measure of a civilization is reflected in its treatment of its weakest segments. So let Israel now build a network of supports for its children and adults with disabilities of which it can feel proud.[24]

In late February 2000, Herr went to the Gaza strip to give a keynote speech on Israeli-Palestinian cooperation in joint work for the rehabilitation of disabled people. It gave him special satisfaction to recall his White House memo calling for just such cooperation. Gaza has the highest population density in world; it is "a tinderbox." "When you cross the border and enter Palestinian protection you're surrounded by smiling, welcoming, machine gun-toting security forces." Yasir Arafat's brother Fahti told Herr, "I'd like to keep you all for a few days. I'd like for us to be singing and dancing together, not just sharing ideas." Herr saw that Palestinian land is arid, while the Israeli settlements control the best areas, including the beach front. He was ruefully reminded of Cherokee; here with a couple of million "penned up" Palestinians, he was once again offered an opportunity to share without condescension.

Herr always has a dozen projects before him. He juggles them successfully, he believes, because "the line between work and play is blurred for me. I like reaching out to people in need like Elvira Walkingstick whose house in Cherokee I'd gotten water to. I like being off the beaten track. I look at some of the conventional lawyers who are bored and think of how excited I am every day."[25]

*   *   *   *   *   *   *

When four Bronx policemen shot African immigrant Amadou Diallo in February 1999, many New Yorkers were shaken with sorrow and anger. Every citizen, even the policemen themselves, regretted the incident, but only some felt that the shooting reflected both the subconscious racism of large numbers of police officers, both in the city and throughout the nation, and the hostile posture of the city's mayor, Rudy Giuliani. A month of sit-down protests in front of the police administration building was as much a demand for changed police policy and behavior as it was for criminal indictments against the four officers.

Rabbi Sharon Kleinbaum of Congregation Beth Simchat Torah, Greenwich Village's organized gay and lesbian synagogue, felt that New York's Jewish community must have a visible part in the sit-down protests. She was one of a group of 15 rabbis, calling themselves Jews for Racial and Economic Justice, who arranged to be arrested together on one day of the protest. It was hardly her first act of civil disobedience. She had already been arrested a dozen times before, but this was the first time in 18 years. It was 19 years since she had seen the sugar plantations of Jeannerette, Louisiana and had been inspired by the militant dynamism of Sister Anne Catherine.

As with Fred Nathan, Sharon Kleinbaum's involvement with the AJSS was a family legacy. Her father Max was not only a founding member of the organization's Board of Directors, but he was a protégé of Isidor Hoffman, like his mentor committed to righteous activity as the defining characteristic of his Judaism.

Born in the Bronx in 1913 and raised in the Shalom Alechem Housing Projects (a left-wing housing cooperative), Max Kleinbaum was profoundly moved by the Sacco & Vanzetti case, talking about it with each of the four children he raised. Kleinbaum went to the New York School of Social Work where he met and was awed by Isidor Hoffman, despite Max's own totally secular upbringing and orientation. Max was a founder of the Jewish Peace Fellowship and a conscientious objector during World War II. Kleinbaum's life was based on Jewish communal work. He worked with the Jewish Welfare Board; his view was that the Jewish community must be a force for good. During the war he earned his non-combatant status by serving as a social worker in psychiatric hospitals. Sharon was taught that what one does as a Jew in life is to live for others, not by giving lectures, but by living a life of righteousness. Isidor Hoffman married Sharon's parents. Her father's advancing age led him to retire from the AJSS board in the late 1970s.

Sharon was introduced to activism by her older brothers (she is the last of four children and the only female). The family visited the AJSS projects her brothers attended. As a nine-year-old she canvassed for Gene McCarthy in 1968. Her oldest brother, a conscientious objector during the Vietnam war, worked for the United Farm Workers during the boycott days; she picketed supermarkets. Sharon never attended AJSS as a camper because the summer she was 16 she had become Orthodox, and she could not travel on Saturdays.

Her Orthodoxy had not been anticipated by her parents or by herself. Because of the deteriorating public schools in Rutherford, New Jersey- each of her brothers went to the public high school there and her parents were increasingly dissatisfied – Sharon was sent to the Orthodox high school in the community from 1973-1977. The school had already been affected by the women's movement and allowed girls to partake in religious study. Sharon found a depth of intellectual thought to match her social activism; this gave her a way of understanding her Judaism.

Her feminism and her awareness of herself as gay made it clear to her that Orthodoxy was not her path. She was attracted to a variety of radical politics: against nuclear weapons, for tenants rights, against Apartheid and for the South African divestment movement. She did not see a link between her activism and her Jewish identity until she was hired by Jules and Julianne Hirsh to serve as a counselor in 1980, working under the auspices of the Southern Mutual Help Association.

The AJSS taught her that helping people would become a defining characteristic of her Judaism. Her role as a counselor also made her desire to share this awareness with young people. Before AJSS she had a bifurcated consciousness: a devout Jewish religious life and a politically active college life. AJSS united her interests, translating Judaism into action. She was particularly inspired to see the transformation of unthinking suburbanite campers into caring human beings. "You cannot help being a different person when you see one person, Sister Anne Catherine, dedicate her life to changing the world."

Following her AJSS summer, Kleinbaum became committed to the War Resisters League, participating in civil disobedience in West Virginia against the placement of Pershing missles in Europe; she was arrested at Pentagon sit-ins many times. She walked from Copenhagen to Paris in 1981 with a Scandinavian feminist peace group, arriving in Paris on Hiroshima Day. She stayed in Europe to build the international peace movement, and she organized for Woman's Pentagon Action Days at the Pentagon in November of 1980 and 1981. A European contributor to WIN magazine (the WRL journal), she was asked to return to the United States to help mobilize the massive June 1982 anti-nuclear protest in Central Park. In the aftermath of the demonstration, Kleinbaum participated in sit-ins at the embassies of the then five members of the nuclear club on June 14, 1982.

Engaged in the frenzied pace of political activism, young Sharon had still not melded social action with Jewish action, except for her seven weeks as an AJSS counselor. Attempting to meet that goal, she moved to Amherst to be assistant director of National Yiddish Book Center, where she was surrounded by young, politically active Jewish people.

In 1985 Sharon Kleinbaum entered Reconstructionist Rabbinical College in Philadelphia, becoming one of seven AJSS participants who are now rabbis. Sharon was stimulated by teaching young unaffiliated Jews of the relevancy of a contemporary Judaism to progressive values and an activist life. Convinced that these backgrounds can nourish each other, she adopted the activist rabbi as her career model. The college was progressive, open to dealing with gay students; the year before she entered the administration had decided on a no-discrimination policy on the basis of sexual orientation. In addition to working on gay/straight issues, there was also a progressive faction at the school working on Arab/Jewish issues, seeking to make Israel a just place for all of its inhabitants. She explored the question of how to open Judaism to gay families. She ran workshops and led panel discussions, trying to discover how to make different people and different families comfortable.

While a student she spent a year in Israel, working with the Rabbinical Human Rights organization to demand an end to occupation of the territories.

After graduation she went to Washington in 1990 to work for the Religious Action Center of Reform Judaism, doing federal lobbying and seeking better black-Jewish communication. She was the Director of Congregational Relations and a liaison to 850 synagogues. Her job was to teach temple leaders how to integrate social action into their agendas- e.g. how to do a discussion of gun control. She created a literature bank on Judaism and social justice. "It is a rich Jewish tradition, not just a product of western democratic values." She did this for two years, until 1992. She was approached about her present job and was warned that it was "too risky," that leading a gay synagogue would be professional suicide. But Kleinbaum felt, "I'm a risk taker."

"I learned from my parents when I was very young," Kleinbaum told the *New York Times* in 1993, "that if you let people who hate you define you, you can't get by in the world. You can't let the negative define who you are." *Times* reporter Alex Withcel added, "It certainly hasn't defined Rabbi Kleinbaum, who at 33 is undeterred in her quest for an inclusive Judaism."[26]

As Kleinbaum sees it, the first task of her rabbinate is to mend the "brokenness" of so many gay Jews and then to participate in political actions in leading a righteous life.

She was named in the spring of 2000 by the Jewish Fund for Social Justice as one of three women of valor. She's initiated a dialogue with the Unity Fellowship Church, a non-denominational gay church in the Fort Greene section of Brooklyn. She works for the New Israeli Fund, which advocates progressive Israeli politics on battered woman's issues, more complete social services, and Arab-Jewish relations so as to strengthen domestic values in Israel.

At the center of her pastoral work is comforting those with AIDS, and she is a prominent advocate for funds and research, especially for, though not limited to, the Gay Men's Health Crisis organization. She consulted with officials of the US Holocaust Museum, helping to plan the exhibit which recognizes Nazi atrocities against homosexuals.

Kleinbaum is a member of the National Religious Leadership Round Table, which plans events countering the efforts of the religious right. The group holds public meetings and panel discussions in areas where Christian conservatives are strong to counter the idea that they speak God's word on social issues.[27]

Kleinbaum has defined her work in synagogue in passionate language:

> How do you mend a broken world? How can we live through the brokenness? How do we get past the feeling that we are caught in the midst of a second *Mabool*, a second Flood, whether we experience it as lesbians or gays or women or Jews or as African Americans or people with AIDS or Kosovors – or even as ordinary middle class Americans with a nagging sense that we've gotten just about everything we could ever really want in life except the sense of meaning and purpose that would make it all worthwhile? How do we get past the feeling that God has forgotten the covenant with Noah, has forgotten the promise of the rainbow, has forgotten us? We can only do what Noah did: we can build a *tevah*, an ark to help carry us through the Flood of our times, both in a personal sense and also in the larger sense of our lives, the historical and global sense. This ark is community, and Congregation Beth Simchat Torah is such an ark, a spiritual community, in every sense of the word...
>
> I became a rabbi because I believed that a synagogue could create an entirely different kind of religious experience. No one joins CBST in order to impress their grandmother, *bar mitzvah* their child, or increase their prestige at work. People join CBST for the sake of participating in a hardworking, volunteer driven, active and activist religious community. At CBST, we come together to worship, and to determine the best way to send relief to the Kosovors. We pray, and we wrap packages of holiday food and other things to take them to people who are homebound and hospitalized and who could not possibly get to a Passover *Seder* or who would not otherwise have a *menorah* for *Chanukah* or *dreidels, groggers*, and *Hamantashen* for Purim. We study Torah, and visit people with AIDS who have been disowned by their families. We learn Talmud, and support programs for the elderly. We make music, and campaign against discrimination in the workplace. We learn Yiddish, and attend vigils in memory of Mathew Shepard and get ourselves arrested for civil disobedience at protests for Amadou Diallo. This work comes from a deep spiritual commitment, felt individually and acted upon communally, that being Jewish means more than attending High Holy Day services and that being an out lesbian or an out gay man means more than watching the annual Pride Parade. The depth of this commitment is what makes CBST the community that it is: a profoundly spiritual community that is at the same time highly engaged with the world around it.[28]

The satisfaction Kleinbaum derives from her work lead her to tell the *Times*, "I think I'm the luckiest rabbi in America, even though America may not agree."[29]

Nancy Marks, Fred Nathan, Stanley Herr, and Sharon Kleinbaum have made their social commitment central to their daily activity; whether religious or not, they are living the prophetic ideal. Most graduates of the American Jewish Society for Service, of course, do not live professional lives of community service, but hundreds have incorporated the impulse to serve in many of their thoughts and activities. For inspiration, we might turn again to Stanley Herr. One of the many hats he wears bears the logo of American Association on Mental Retardation. He was president of AAMR from 1998-1999. His Presidential address of May 1999 may serve as a credo for all:

> Doing justice is everyone's work. It is not the exclusive province of some profession or the monopoly of the paid public servants we call judges. Each of us is - or can be – a justice worker in our field, community, nation, and throughout the world. In doing so, we must learn from each other, whether our situation is humble or elevated, whether we are supported or a supporter. For, as the Jewish Talmud teaches: "Who is wise? He who learns from every person."[30]

NOTES

CHAPTER ONE

[1] *PM Daily:* 28 July 1940, 12; 29 July 1940, 4; 4 February 1941, 14; 5 August 1941, 15.

[2] Paul Milkman, *PM: A New Deal in Journalism, 1940-1948* (New Brunswick: Rutgers University Press, 1997), 156-157.

[3] Irving Howe, *World of Our Fathers* (New York and London: Harcourt, Brace, Jovanovich, 1976), pp. 287-341.

[4] Joan Micklin Silver, Director *Hester Street*; a Midwest Productions Film. Screenplay by Joan Micklin Silver from the story *Yekl* by Abraham Cahan; 1975.

[5] Reprinted in Abraham Cahan, *Yekl and The Imported Bridegroom and other stories of the New York Ghetto* (New York: Dover Publications, 1970).

[6] Edward S. Shapiro, *A Time for Healing* (Volume V of *The Jewish People in America*), Baltimore and London, The Johns Hopkins University Press, 1992, 145

[7] Deborah Dash Moore, *At Home in America: Second Generation New York Jews* (NY: Columbia U Press, 1981).

[8] Shapiro, 99-101.

[9] Shapiro, 143-145.

[10] Chaim Potok's semi-autobiographical novels, *The Chosen*(New York: 1967) and *The Promised (*New York: 1969) trace the transformation of Brooklyn's orthodox communities into Hassidic strongholds in the period following World War II.

[11] Shapiro, 159. Howe's monumental history records the withering of secular Jewish institutions.

[12] Shapiro, 149-150

[13] Ferdinand M. Isserman, *Opening Statement at Institute of Jewish Theology*, Hebrew Union College, Cincinnati, 29 March 1950.

[14] *Who's Who in American Jewry*

[15] Ferdinand M. Isserman, *Rebels and Saints: The Social Message of the Prophets of Israel* (St. Louis: The Bethany Press, 1933), 127-128.

[16] Ibid, 20.

[17] Ferdinand M. Isserman, *This is Judaism* (Chicago & New York: Willett, Lack & Co., 1944)

[18] *Rebels and Saints*, 20.

[19] *This is Judaism*, 192-193

[20] Ibid., 61.

[21] *Rebels and Saints*, 41-42

[22] Ibid., 106-107.

[23] Revised Standard Holy Bible (New York: Oxford University Press, 1962) *Leviticus* 19:9-10, discussed in *This is Judaism*, 192.

[24] *This is Judaism*, 194.

[25] Ibid., 195.

[26] *Rebels and Saints*, 83-84.

[27] *Leviticus* 19:33-34.

[28] Ferdinand M. Isserman, *Sentenced to Death* (St. Louis, the Modern View Publishing Company, 1933), and Ferdinand M. Isserman, *My Second Visit to Nazi Germany* (Mimeographed), 1935

[29] *Rebels and Saints*, 113.

[30] *This is Judaism*, 183.

[31] Ibid., 222.

[32] Potok, *The Chosen*.

[33] Arthur J. Lelyveld, *The Steadfast Stream* (Cleveland: Pilgrim Press, 1995), 1-6 *passim*.

[34] Ibid., 64.

[35] Lawrence Van Gelder, "Rabbi Arthur J. Lelyveld, 83 Rights Crusader," *New York Times*, 16 April 1996, B7.

[36] New York Times, 29 January 1981.

[37] Michael Young, "Facing a Test of Faith: Jewish Pacifists During the Second World War," and Rob Polner, "Rabbi Hoffman: Pacifist and Jew," in Murray Polner and Naomi Goldman, Editors, The Challenge of Shalom: The Jewish Tradition of Peace and Justice (Philadelphia, Pennsylvania, and Gabriola Island, British Columbia: New Society Publishers, 1994) 156-167, 222-224.

[38] *The Steadfast Stream*, 14

[39] *The Gospel According to St. Mathew*, 5:3-10

[40] *Rebels and Prophets*, 138-140.

[41] Howard H. Brinton, *Friends for 300 Years* (Wallingford, Pa: Pendle Hill Publications, 1952, 1964), 118

[42] Gerald Jonas, *On Doing Good: The Quaker Experiment* (New York: Scribner's, 1971) 19

[43] Brinton, 36.

[44] Jonas, 27.

[45] John Woolman, *A Plea for the Poor* (1763), quoted by Jonas, 70.

[46] Brinton, 147.

[47] Jonas, 14-15.

[48] Jonas 85-139; Mary Hoxie Jones, *Swords Into Ploughshares* (Westport Connecticut, Greenpoint Press, 1971 reprint of New York: Macmillan, 1937); Marvin R. Weisbord, *Some Form of Peace: True Stories of the American Friends Service Committee* (New York: Viking, 1968).

[49] Jonas, 211.

[50] Ibid., 202-229

[51] Weisbord, 105-125.

[52] Henry Kohn, interviews with the author, 22 August 1998 (Rhinebeck, New York), 13 October 1998 (New York, New York). Telephone interviews 31 March 2000 (New York and Brooklyn) and 2 April 2000 (Rhinebeck and Brooklyn). I was also permitted to see an unpublished memoir of Henry Kohn written for his family.

CHAPTER TWO

[1] Interviews with Henry Kohn, New York City, 13 October 1998, 27 January, 1999.

[2] Records of the American Jewish Society for Service, Manuscript Group 1495, Manuscripts

and Archives, Sterling Memorial Library, Yale University [Hereafter referred to as AJSS Archives] , Box 1.

³ Interviews with Henry Kohn; AJSS Archives , Box 1

⁴ American Friends Service Committee Archives

⁵ Melvyn Dobofsky, Athan Theoharis, and Daniel M. Smith, *The United States in the Twentieth Century* (Englewood Cliffs, NJ: Prentice-Hall, 1978), 363.

⁶ Ibid. 149.

⁷ Irwin Stark, "Jewish Work-Camp in Indianapolis, *Commentary*, 13:1 (January 1952), 9. The quotation from *Survey Graphic* is not documented.

⁸ Ibid.

⁹ There's a funnier variation on this theme. It is the story of the solitary survivor of a shipwreck, found alone on an island after ten years. Before he departs, he proudly illustrates the mini-civilization he created: He has built three impressive edifices. He identifies the first as his home and the second as his temple. When asked about the third, he shifts from pride to contempt. "That temple... That temple I wouldn't even set foot in!"

¹⁰ E-mail from Paul Doudna to the author, 11 November 1998.

¹¹ Ibid.

¹² Stark, "Jewish Work-Camp", 10.

¹³ AJSS Archives, Box 1.

¹⁴ Irwin and Alice Stark, "Directors' Report on the First Work Camp of the American Jewish Society for Service at Flanner House, Indianapolis, Indiana", 2, in AJSS Archives, Box 1.

¹⁵ Ibid.

¹⁶ AJSS Archives, Box 1 Folder 6.

¹⁷ AJSS Archives, Box 2 Folder 7.

¹⁸ AJSS Archives, Box 1 Folder 6.

¹⁹ Ibid.

²⁰ AJSS Archives, Box 2 Folder 7.

²¹ AJSS Archives Box 2 Folder 16.

²² Ibid.

²³ Interview with Henry Kohn, 27 January 1999.

²⁴ Howe, 287-314, 518-551, 598-607, 634-638.

²⁵ American Friends Service Committee, Handbook for Project Leaders, 1953 in AJSS Archives, Box 2 Folder 12.

²⁶ AJSS Archives; Box 2, Folders 14-21.

²⁷ "Kids Help Food Area and Love it; Students Work at Winsted," *New York World-Telegram and Sun*, 21 July, 1956.

²⁸ Telephone Interview with Michael Clarke, Sarasota, Florida and Brooklyn, New York, 26 May 1999.

²⁹ *New York World-Telegram and Sun*, 27 March 1957.

³⁰ *Springfield (Ohio) Sun*, 13 August 1957; Dayton Daily News, 7 July 1957.

³¹ AJSS Archives, Box 3, Folders 22-25.

CHAPTER THREE

¹ Edmund S. Morgan, *American Slavery, American Freedom: The Ordeal of Virginia* (New York: Norton, 1975).

[2] W.E.B. DuBois, *The Souls of Black Folk* (Greenwich, Connecticut: Fawcett Publications, 1961), 23. Originally published in 1903.

[3] Stark, "Jewish Work-Camp in Indianapolis," 11-12.

[4] Ibid. 12.

[5] Taylor Branch, *Parting the Waters: America in the King Years, 1954-1963* (New York: Simon and Schuster, 1988), 121.

[6] Ibid. 121-122, 130, 207, 263-264, 289-290, 310, 381, 486-487.

[7] Interview with Henry Kohn, Marquette Michigan, 21 July 1999.

[8] Telephone Interview with Michael Clarke, Sarasota, Florida and Brooklyn, New York, 26 May 1999.

[9] Elly Saltzman, "American Jewish Society for Service Work Camp, Frogmore, South Carolina, July 1st – August 16th, 1959," 1-3. The report and other documents of this summer are in AJSS Archives, Box 3, Folder 28.

[10] Interview with Henry Kohn, Marquette, Michigan, 21 July 1999.

[11] Saltzman, Frogmire, South Carolina Report, 2.

[12] Interview with Ed Cohen, Long Beach, Long Island, 9 June 1999.

[13] Ed Cohen, Project Director's Report, 1962 Project in Indianapolis, AJSS Archives Box 4, Folder 38.

[14] Interview with Ed Cohen.

[15] Nathan Glazer and Daniel Patrick Moynihan, *Beyond the Melting Pot: The Negroes, Puerto Ricans, Jews, Italians and Irish of New York City* (Cambridge: The M.I.T. Press, 1963) pp. 71-77.

[16] Ibid.

[17] Ed Cohen, Project Director's Report. 1962 Indianapolis, Indiana.

[18] CBS Reports, *The Hate That Hate Produced*, 1959.

[19] Regina H. Saxton, Letter to 1962 Palatine, Illinois AJSS, 2 August 1962, submitted with Jules and Julianne Hirsh, 1962 Project Directors' Report.

[20] I directed the 1993 Selma, Alabama project.

[21] Interview with Rhonda Kirschner, New York City, 2 June 1999.

[22] Jules and Julianne Hirsh, Project Directors' Report, Clinton, Kentucky, 1968; Kirschner interview.

[23] Ibid.

[24] Interview with Jules and Julianne Hirsh, 10 March 1999, Brooklyn, New York.

[25] Ibid.

[26] Jules and Julianne Hirsh, Project Directors' Report, Hattiesburg, Mississippi, 1978.

[27] Ibid.

[28] Jules and Julianne Hirsh, Project Directors' Report, Waterloo, Iowa, 1972.

[29] John Steinbeck, *The Grapes of Wrath,* (New York: Penguin, 1984 [originally 1939]), 332.

[30] Interview with Martin and Rochelle Kopelowitz, East Meadow, New York, 2 April, 1999.

[31] Michael Kaplan and Rachel Frankel, "A Service Excerpt,"in *AJSS 1978 SEMCA* (Camper Newsletter), 7

[32] Jules and Julianne Hirsh, Project Directors' Report, Alice Texas, 1979.

[33] Ruth Sod, untitled, *Chai Times* (1979 Alice Texas Project Newsletter), 25.

[34] Interview with Jules and Julianne Hirsh.

[35] Ibid. See also Jules and Julianne Hirsh, Project Directors' Report, Lewiston North Carolina, 1982.

[36] Interview with Martin and Rochelle Kopelowitz.

[37] Interview with Jules and Julianne Hirsh.

[38] Interview with Carl and Audrey Brenner.

[39] Interview with Martin and Rochelle Kopelowitz.

[40] Jules and Julianne Hirsh, Project Directors' Report, 1984 Dahlonega, Georgia.

[41] Rochelle and Martin Kopelowitz, Project Directors' Report, 1990.

[42] Interview with Martin and Rochelle Kopelowitz.

[43] Ibid.

[44] Jules and Julianne Hirsh, Project Directors' Report, Abbeville, Louisiana, 1971.

[45] *Ms. Magazine* I:7 (January, 1973), 47.

[46] Julianne Hirsh, "To the Crookston Ten" in 1973 Crookston, Minnesota Project newsletter.

[47] Interview with Jules and Julianne Hirsh.

[48] Beth David, untitled poem in *Murph's Here!* (1971 Project Newsletter)

[49] Telephone interview with Henry Kohn, New York, New York, and Brooklyn, New York, 26 May 1999.

[50] Jules and Julianne Hirsh, Project Directors' Report, Abbeville, Louisiana, 1971; interview with Jules and Julianne Hirsh.

[51] Interview with Martin and Rochelle Kopelowitz.

[52] Interview with Jules and Julianne Hirsh.

[53] Interview with Rabbi Sharon Kleinbaum, Brooklyn, New York, 7 June 1999.

[54] Sister Anne Catherine, Talk before AJSS fall meeting, reprinted in December 1992 AJSS Brochure.

[55] Ibid.

CHAPTER FOUR

[1] "American Indians" will be the term used here. "Native Americans" is a linguistic maneuver that doesn't quite work. "American" is a word derived from the name of a European explorer; "native" implies that the population evolved here, whereas most anthropologists believe the people who lived in North and South America when the Europeans arrived crossed over the Bering Straight from northeast Asia between 40,000 and 100,000 years ago. See U.S. Commission on Human Rights, "A Historical Context for Evaluation," (1981), reprinted in Fremont J. Lyden and Lyman T. Legters, editors, *North Americans and Public Policy*, (University of Pittsburgh Press, 1992). Historians sympathetic to this continent's first people and political activists like the American Indian Movement have accepted the old term, regardless of its imperfections.

[2] Ibid. 14.

[3] Ibid. 18

[4] Ibid. 20; Fergus M. Bordewich, *Killing the White Man's Indian* (New York: Doubleday, 1996), 39-48, 55-59.

[5] Dee Brown, *Bury My Heart at Wounded Knee* (New York, Holt, 1970); Peter Matthiessen, *In the Spirit of Crazy Horse* (New York, Viking, 1983), 20-21.

[6] Bordewich, 50-53.

[7] Matthiessen, 6; Bordewich, 179.

[8] US Commission on Human Rights, 21.

[9] Alvin M. Josephy, Jr., *Now That the Buffalo's Gone: A Study of Today's American Indians* (New York: Knopf, 1982), 85. See also Matthiessen, 21, Brown, *passim*.

[10] David Wallace Adams, *Education for Extinction: American Indians and the Boarding School Experience, 1875-1928*, (Lawrence: University Press of Kansas, 1995); H. Guillermo Bartelt, "Boarding School Language Policy and the Spread of English Among Indians of the American Southwest," in Lyden and Legters, 137-146.

[11] Duane Champagne, "Organizational Change and Conflict: A Case Study of the Bureau of Indian Affairs," (1983), reprinted in Lyden and Legters, 33-61; Bordewich, 14; Matthiessen, 27-31.

[12] Telephone interview with Henry Kohn, New York and Brooklyn, 22 September, 1999.

[13] Interview with Ed Cohen.

[14] Stanley Herr letter to Henry Kohn, reprinted in January 1964 AJSS Newsletter.

[15] Jules and Julianne Hirsh, Project Directors' Report, Oglala South Dakota, 1963.

[16] Ibid.

[17] Interview with Jules and Julianne Hirsh.

[18] Interview with Jules and Julianne Hirsh; interview with Elly and Ruth Saltzman, New York, 13 June 1999.

[19] Quoted by Matthiessen, 17.

[20] Matthiessen, 9, 18-19.

[21] Matthiessen, 21.

[22] Ibid. 26.

[23] Interview with Ed Cohen.

[24] Ed Cohen, Project Director's Report, Rosebud Reservation, South Dakota, 1964; interview with Ed Cohen

[25] Josephy, 177-211; Matthiessen, 36.

[26] Carl and Audrey Brenner, Project Directors' Report, Sisseton, South Dakota, 1974.

[27] David B. Weber, letter to Henry Kohn, reprinted in March 1974 AJSS Newsletter.

[28] Martin and Rochelle Kopelowitz, Project Directors' Report, Fort Thompson, South Dakota, 1985.

[29] Interview with Martin and Rochelle Kopelowitz; Martin and Rochelle Kopelowitz, Project Directors' Report, Fort Thompson, South Dakota, 1985.

[30] Letters of anonymous South Dakota campers printed in January 1986 AJSS Newsletter.

[31] Jules and Julianne Hirsh, Project Directors' Report, Cloquet, Minnesota, 1964.

[32] Artie Mayer letter to Henry Kohn, reprinted in March 1965 AJSS Newsletter.

[33] Interview with Carl and Audrey Brenner.

[34] Deborah Pope, "Hole Digger Post" (Project Newsletter), reprinted in AJSS Newsletter, February 1969.

[35] Larry Green in "Hole Digger Post," reprinted in AJSS Newsletter, February 1969.

[36] Jules and Julianne Hirsh, Project Directors' Report, Crow Agency, Montana, 1969.

[37] Interviews with Jules and Julianne Hirsh and Carl and Audrey Brenner.

[38] Arthur Janovsky, *Ahushta Chilaba* (Crow Agency Project Newsletter).

[39] Jules and Julianne Hirsh, Project Directors' Report, Cloquet, Minnesota; Interview with Jules and Julianne Hirsh

[40] Christina Gullion, Letter to Jules Hirsh, reprinted in March 1965 AJSS Newsletter.

[41] Ruth and Elly Saltzman, Project Directors' Report, Steamboat Canyon, Arizona, 1969

[42] Becky Srole, "I Saw" reprinted in February 1970 AJSS Newsletter.

[43] Jules and Julianne Hirsh, Project Directors' Report, Crownpoint, New Mexico, 1967

[44] Alice Fay in *Yah Ta Hey,* 1967 Project Newsletter.

[45] Ruth Obernbreit in *Yah Ta Hey*.

[46] Andrea Edson and Patti-Lou Schultz in *Yah Ta Hey.*

[47] Paul and Catherine Milkman, Project Directors' Report, Wyoming, 1998, in AJSS Project Newsletter, December 1998.

CHAPTER FIVE

[1] Dubofsky, Theoharis, and Smith, 415.

[2] John Kenneth Galbraith, *The Affluent Society* (Boston: Houghton Mifflin, 1958).

[3] Irving Spiegel "Jewish Unit End Kentucky Mission," *New York Times.* 20 August 1960.

[4] Michael Harrington, *The Other America: Poverty in the United States* (New York: Collier, 1962)

[5] Ibid, 1-14.

[6] Ibid 43-44.

[7] Deborah Sharpe, College Application Essay, reprinted in AJSS Newsletter, February 1970.

[8] Irving Bernstein, *Guns or Butter: The Presidency of Lyndon Johnson* (New York and Oxford: Oxford University Press, 1996), 82-113; see also Vaughn Davis Bornet, *The Presidency of Lyndon B. Johnson* (Lawrence: University Press of Kansas, 1983).

[9] Carl and Audrey Brenner, 1969 Project Directors' Report, Ripley Tennessee.

[10] Jules and Julianne Hirsh, 1969 Project Directors' Report, Clinton Kentucky; interview with Jules and Julianne Hirsh.

[11] Dubofsky, Theoharis, and Smith, 464.

[12] Stanley Karnow, *Vietnam: A History; The First Complete Account of Vietnam at War* (New York: Viking, 1983), 24.

[13] AJSS Newsletters, 1967-1971.

[14] Martin and Rochelle Kopelowitz, 1973 Project Directors' Report, Richmond, Virginia.

[15] Felice Burstein, Clinton, Iowa Project Newsletter, 1975.

[16] Paul and Catherine Milkman, 1994 Project Directors' Report, Eugene, Oregon. The author also relied on his memory for much of the detail here.

[17] Larry Novikoff in *the Bluffton Spiker* (1965 Project Newsletter).

[18] Jacqueline Jones, *The Dispossessed: America's Underclass from the Civil War to the Present* (New York: Basic, 1992), 2.

[19] Ed Cohen, 1967 Project Director's Report, Lilbourn, Missouri.

[20] Interview with Carl and Audrey Brenner.

[21] Elly Saltzman, 1971 Project Director's Report, Mora County, New Mexico.

[22] Donna Arzt, 1971 Mora, New Mexico Project Newsletter.

[23] Jones, 172.

[24] Jones, 182.

[25] Ibid. 185.

[26] Paul and Catherine Milkman, 1996 Project Directors' Report, Twin Falls, Idaho.

[27] Alicia Nathan, "All For the Children," 1996 Twin Falls, Idaho Newsletter.

[28] Simone Isturis in 1996 Twin Falls, Idaho Newsletter.

[29] Jones, 198.

[30] Carl and Audrey Brenner, 1970 Project Directors' Report, Alamo, Texas.

[31] David Giber, AJSS Newsletter, February 1971.

[32] Jules and Julianne Hirsh, 1983 Project Directors' Report, McAllen Texas; interview with Jules and Julianne Hirsh.

[33] Jesse Halpern, 1997 Project Newsletter, McAllen Texas.

[34] Paul and Catherine Milkman, 1997 Project Directors' Report, McAllen Texas; 1997 Project Newsletter, McAllen Texas.

[35] Check the index for history on the website www.habitat.org.

[36] Ibid.

[37] Jonathan Hirsh and Karin Kaiser, 1999 Project Directors' Report, Albany Georgia.

CHAPTER SIX

[1] Deborah Dash Moore, *At Home in America: Second Generation New York Jews* (NY: Columbia U Press, 1981.

[2] AJSS archives.

[3] Moore, Howe.

[4] Marshall Sklare, "The Sociology of the American Synagogue," (1971) in Jacob Neusner, editor, *Understanding American Judaism: Toward the Description of a Modern Religion* (New York: Ktav Publishing House, 1975), 93.

[5] Charles S. Liebman, "The Religion of American Jews" (1973) in Neusner, 33.

[6] AJSS archives, 1964 correspondence.

[7] Interview with Carl and Audrey Brenner.

[8] Marshall Sklare and Joseph Greenblum, *Jewish Identity on the Suburban Frontier: A Study of Group Survival in the Open Society* (New York: Basic, 1967), 50-55. See also Arthur Hertzberg, "The American Jew and His Religion" (1964) in Neusner; Jack Wetheimer, *A People Divided: Judaism in Contemporary America* (New York: Basic, 1993); Deborah Dash Moore, *To the Golden Cities: Pursuing the American Jewish Dream in Miami and L.A.* (New York: The Free Press, 1994).

[9] Sklare, *Jewish Identity*, 62.

[10] Hertzberg, in Neusner, 5-6.

[11] Wertheimer, 4.

[12] Cited by Wertheimer, 59.

[13] Conversations with my campers must remain confidential, but intellectually restless Jewish day school students have shared their beliefs in private conversations and at project services in 1993, 1994, 1998, and 1999.

[14] Sklare and Greenblum, *Jewish Identity*, xii.

[15] Interview with Ed Cohen.

[16] Stanley Herr letter to Henry Kohn, reprinted in January 1964 AJSS Newsletter.

[17] Arthur Lifson and Henry Kohn in December 1997 AJSS Newsletter.

[18] Elly and Ruth Saltzman, 1962 Project Directors' Report, Haifa Israel, in AJSS Archives.

[19] AJSS Newsletters, 1961-1969.

[20] AJSS Newsletters 1963-1999.

[21] Interview with Ed Cohen.

[22] Interview with Jules and Julianne Hirsh.

[23] Interview with Carl and Audrey Brenner.

[24] Interviews with Carl and Audrey Brenner, Jules and Julianne Hirsh, and Martin and Rochelle Kopelowitz.

[25] Julianne Hirsh in the 1973 Crookston, Minnesota Project Newsletter.

[26] 1971 AJSS Newsletter.

[27] Minutes of the Board of Directors Meetings, 1998 and 1999.

28 Facsimiles of Kohn's telegrams are in the AJSS Archives; Elly Saltzman, 1959 Project Director's Report.

29 Interview with Martin and Rochelle Kopelowitz.

30 Jonathan Hirsh and Karin Kaiser, 1996 Project Directors' Report, Reno and Virginia City, Nevada.

31 AJSS Archives; AJSS Newsletters, 1960-1999.

32 I directed the 1995 project in Aroostook County, Maine.

33 Martin and Rochelle Kopelowitz, 1973 Project Directors' Report, Oregon Hills, Virginia.

34 Telephone interview with Martin Kopelowitz, 24 January 2000.

35 Ibid.

36 Telephone interview with Jonathan Hirsh, 17 January 2000.

37 Ibid.

38 Audrey Brenner letter to the author, 19 January 2000.

39 Jules and Julianne Hirsh, 1974 Project Directors' Report, Tacoma Washington. Telephone interview with Julianne Hirsh, 24 January 2000.

40 Telephone interview with Martin Kopelowitz.

41 Audrey Brenner letter.

EPILOGUE

1 Geneva B. Hamilton, letter to Henry Kohn, 18 April 1984.

2 Sister Anne Catherine Bizalion to Henry Kohn, 8 May 1984.

3 Joseph Jefferson to Henry Kohn, May 1984.

4 1999 AJSS brochure.

5 Interview with Nancy Marks, New York City, 7 February 2000.

6 Stephen Killian letter to AJSS office, Fall 1999 (undated).

7 Lorna Bourg, Executive Director, Southern Mutual Help Association, letter to Henry Kohn, 16 December, 1999.

8 Janna Cohen-Rosenthal letter to AJSS office, Fall 1999 (undated).

9 Elizabeth Brody letter to AJSS office, Fall 1999 (undated).

10 Michael Steele letter to AJSS office, Fall 1999 (undated).

11 Michael Kaplan letter to AJSS office, Fall 1999 (undated).

12 Ann Hirsh Greenhill letter to AJSS office, Fall 1999 (undated).

13 Jane Plitt letter to AJSS office, Fall 1999 (undated).

14 Andrea Avrutis letter to AJSS office, Fall 1999 (undated).

15 Julie Pulenwitz letter to AJSS office, Fall 1999 (undated).

16 Interview with Fred Nathan, 18 February 2000.

17 Audrey and Carl Brenner, 1977 Project Directors' Report, San Miguel, New Mexico.

18 Ibid.

19 Fred Nathan in *Think New Mexico: A Solution-Oriented Think Tank Serving New Mexicans,* Fall 1999.

20 "Full-day Kindergarten is a sound investment," *Albuquerque Tribune,* 1 September 1999; "Full-day Kindergarten: It's About Time," *Santa Fe New Mexican,* 30 August 1999; Mark Oswald, "All-day kindergarten," *Santa Fe New Mexican,* 31 August 1999; "Who wants full-day kindergarten? A New Mexico think tank has launched an aggressive campaign in the state legislature" by Anne Constable, *Santa fe Reporter,* 26 January- 1 February 2000; "A good kindergarten plan and a way to pay for it," *Albuquerque Tribune,* 6 January 2000;

"New Mexico's young leaders: Fred Nathan, 37: Founder, Think New Mexico," *The New Mexican*, 2 May 1999, A-8.

[21] *Santa Fe New Mexican*, 11 March 2000; *Santa Fe Reporter*, 15-21 March 2000; *Albuquerque Journal*, 9 March 2000.

[22] Interview with Fred Nathan.

[23] Telephone interview with Stanley Herr, Haifa, Israel, and Brooklyn, 29 February 2000.

[24] Stanley Herr, e-mail to the author 5 March, 2000.

[25] Telephone interview with Stanley Herr.

[26] Alex Witchel, " 'Luckiest Rabbi in America,' Holds Faith Amid the Hate," *New York Times*, 5 May 1993, p. C1, C12.

[27] Interviews with Sharon Kleinbaum, Brooklyn, New York, 7 June 1999 and 28 February 2000.

[28] Sharon Kleinbaum, *Synagogue As Spiritual Community: Congregation Beth Simchat Torah* (printed by CBST, 1999).

[29] Witchel, *New York Times*.

[30] Stanley Herr, "Perspectives: Presidential Address 1999 – Working for Justice: Responsibilities for the Next Millennium" in *Mental Retardation*, October 1999, 408.

Appendix: AJSS Project Hosts
(1951-2000)

Year	City, State	Host
1951	Indianapolis, IN	Flanner House
1952	Winchester, NH	Camp Forest Lake
1953	Northfield, MA	Camp Forest Lake and Rabbit Hollow (Winchester, NH)
	Hawthorne, NY	HawthorneCedar Knolls (Fed. Supported)
1954	Morgantown, WV	State of West Virginia
	Fallsington, PA	Penn Valley Community Center
1955	Monteagle, TN	Highlander Folk School
1956	Winsted, CT	City of Winsted
1957	Yellow Springs, OH	Antioch College (Glen Helen Preserve)
1958	Pottstown, PA	Fellowship House Farm
1959	Frogmore, SC	Penn Community Services
1960	Buckhorn, KY	Presbyterian Child Welfare Agency
1961	Pierre, SD	Boys' Club of America (Local)
	Palatine, IL	Camp Reinberg
1962	Palatine, IL	Camp Reinberg
	Indianapolis, IN	Flanner House
	Kiryat Haim, Israel	Israel Guide Dog Foundation for the Blind
1963	Pine Ridge, SD	Pine Ridge Sioux Reservation
	Pine Ridge, SD	Oglala Youth Camp
	Cherokee, NC	U.S. Public Health Service
1964	Rosebud, SD	Rosebud Sioux Reservation
	Cloquet, MN	Fond Du Lac Chippewa Reservation
	Macy, NE	Omaha Reservation
1965	Albuquerque, NM	Barelas Community Center (City of Albuquerque)
	Palatine, IL	Camp Reinberg
	Bluffton, OH	Allen-Hancock Disaster Committee
1966	Toledo, OH	Migrant Reception Center
	Babb, MT	Blackfeet Reservation
	East Troy, WI	Hull House Association

1967	Lilbourn, MO	Delmo Housing Corp.
	Crownpoint, NM	Crownpoint Community Association and Bureau of Indian Affairs
	Lackawana, NY	Tenants' Action Committee
1968	Northern Cheyenne, MT	Northern Cheyenne Reservation
	Clinton, KY	Community Action Program
	Fort Duchesne, UT	Ute Reservation
1969	Steamboat Canyon, AZ	Navajo Reservation
	Crow Agency, MT	Crow Reservation
	Ripley, TN	Office of Economic Development
1970	McAllen, TX	United Farm Workers Union and Mercedes Renewal Program
	Seaford, DE	Community Action Program of Sussex County (O.E.O.)
	Fulton, KY	Mississippi River Economic Opportunity Council
1971	Abbeville, LA	Southern Mutual Help Association
	Madisonville, KY	Hopkins-Muhlenberg Community Action Agency
	Woodburn, OR	Valley Migrant League of Woodburn
	Mora, NM	New Mexico Welfare Department
1972	Tahlequah, OK	International Basic Economy Corporation Indian Housing Program
	Abbeville, LA	Southern Mutual Help Association
	Waterloo, IA	Operation Threshold
	Lewes, DE	Community Action Agency of Sussex County (O.E.O.)
1973	Crookston, MN	Tri-Valley Opportunity Council (O.E.O.)
	Sisseton, SD	Northeast South Dakota Community Action Program
	Westmore, VT	Orleans County Council of Service Agencies
	Richmond, VA	The Oregon Hill Home Improvement Corporation
1974	Opelika, AL	Alabama Council of Human Relations
	Orland, ME	The Homeworkers Organized of More Employment
	Tacoma, WA	Urban League
1975	Spokane, WA	The House of Solomon; The Washington-Alaska Regional Medical Program; and Housing Information Council

	Greenville, NC	Greenville Ministerial Association
	Clinton, IA	Iowa East Central TRAIN (Teach, Rehabilitate and Aid Iowa's Needy)
1976	Rochester, NY	Brown Square Development Corporation
	Grand Rapids, MI	Catholic Human Development Office
	Charlottesville, VA	Charlottesville Housing Improvement Program
1977	Springfield, MA	Old Hill Neighbors, Inc.
	Madison, WI	Freedom House
	Las Cruces, NM	Councilio Campesino del Sudoeste
1978	Hattiesburg, MS	South East Mississippi Community Action Agency
	Des Moines, IA	The Housing Action Alliance
	Lincoln, NE	South Salt Creek Community Organization
1979	Wake Forest, NC	Town of Wake Forest, Community Development Project—1979
	Alice, TX	Rural Economic Assistance League; Community Action Corporation of South Texas; and Jewish Community Council of Corpus Christi
1980	Goldsboro, NC	Operation Bootstrap
	Jeanerette, LA	Southern Mutual Help Association
1981	Hinckley, ME	Hinckley Home School Farm
	Eustis, FL	Lake Community Development Inc.
1982	Cannelton, IN	Historic Cannelton, Inc.
	Lewiston, NC	Mount Olive Baptist Church
1983	Des Moines, IA	Neighborhood Housing Services of Des Moines
	Edinburg, TX	Hidalgo County Economic Development Agency
1984	Jackson, MS	Mississippi Food Network
	Dahlonega, GA	Help in Housing of Lumpkin County
1985	Fort Thompson, SD	Crow Creek Sioux Tribe
	Amarillo, TX	Amarillo Habitat for Humanity
1986	Cincinnati, OH	Neighborhood Housing Services
	Marty, SD	Yankton Sioux Tribe
1987	Cumberland, MD	Interfaith Consortium of Greater Cumberland
	St. Louis, MO	St. Louis Habitat for Humanity
1988	Denton, MD	Maryland Rural Development Corporation

	Laredo, TX	Laredo-Webb County Community Action Agency
1989	Florence, SC	Peedee Community Action Agency
	Chattanooga, TN	Chattanooga Neighborhood Enterprise
1990	Wilmington, DE	Interfaith Housing Task Force
	Detroit, MI	Neighborhood East Area Residents
1991	Chicago, IL	Chicago-Rosebud Coalition for Community Control and Dearborn Homes Resident Management Corp.
	Topeka, KS	Cornerstone of Topeka
	Everett, WA	Housing Hope
1992	Four Corners, LA	Southern Mutual Help Association
	Fabens, TX	Lower Valley Housing Corporation
1993	Selma, AL	Selma Habitat for Humanity
	Fabens, TX	Lower Valley Housing Corporation
	Eugene, OR	Eugene Emergency Housing
1994	Grand Forks, ND	Quad County Community Action Agency
	Phoenix, AZ	Community Housing Partnership
	Eugene, OR	Society of St. Vincent DePaul
1995	Caribou, ME	Catholic Charities Maine and the Town of Fort Fairfield
	Tulsa, OK	Project Get-Together
	Tucson, AZ	Tucson Metropolitan Ministry
1996	Tulsa, OK	Project Get-Together
	Twin Falls, ID	Idaho Migrant Council
	Virginia City, NV	Community Chest
1997	Milwaukee, WI	Milwaukee Community Service Corp.
	McAllen, TX	Rio Grande Habitat for Humanity
	Salt Lake City, UT	Life Care (S.L.C. Community Services Council)
1998	Kansas City, KS	Kaw Valley Habitat for Humanity
	Tulsa, OK	Community Action Project of Tulsa County (Formerly Project Get-Together)
	Riverton/Casper, WY	Riverton Habitat for Humanity and Casper Habitat for Humanity
1999	Albany, GA	Flint River Habitat for Humanity
	Marquette, MI	Marquette Habitat for Humanity
	Escanaba, MI	Bay De Noc Habitat for Humanity

2000	Helena, MT	Helena Habitat for Humanity
	Riverton, WY	Riverton Habitat for Humanity and Housing Partners
	Santa Ana, CA	Orange County Habitat for Humanity

INDEX